Fundraising and Friend-Raising on the Web

Adam Corson-Finnerty
Laura Blanchard

American Library Association
Chicago and London 1998

Project editor: Louise D. Howe

Cover design by Richmond Jones

Text design by Dianne M. Rooney

Composition by the dotted i in Berkeley using QuarkXPress v. 3.32

Printed on 60-pound White Offset, a pH-neutral stock, and bound in 12-point coated cover stock by Data Reproductions

The paper used in this publication meets the minimum requirements of American National Standard for Information Sciences—Permanence of Paper for Printed Library Materials, ANSI Z39.48-1992. ∞

Library of Congress Cataloging-in-Publication Data
Corson-Finnerty, Adam Daniel.
    Fundraising and friend-raising on the Web / Adam Corson-Finnerty
and Laura Blanchard.
        p.   cm.
    Includes index.
    ISBN 0-8389-0727-X (alk. paper)
    1. Library fund raising—United States—Computer network resources.
    2. Electronic fund raising—United States.   3. World Wide Web (Information
retrieval system)   I. Blanchard, Laura.   II. Title.
    Z683.2.U6C67   1998
    025.1′1—dc21   97-51833

02   01   00   99   98   5   4   3   2   1

To our spouses—
Susan Corson-Finnerty
and
Roy Blanchard

Contents

Preface

Fundraising and friend-raising with the World Wide Web combine both science and art—and in an unpredictable and often delightful mixture. There is an old saw that says that fundraising is not gimmicks, stratagems, or clever ploys. Fundraising, this adage goes, "is sitting next to someone and getting them to write you a check." We agree.

Can "virtual" fundraising replace face-to-face fundraising? Can a fundraiser "sit next to someone" in cyberspace? Will cybercash replace greenbacks? The answers to these three questions are no, yes, and time will tell.

The development team at the University of Pennsylvania Library has been using the Web since 1995 for public relations, constituency-building, and the solicitation of gifts. Since "wired" libraries have excellent storefront locations on the information boulevard, we have never wavered in our conviction that the Internet and its friendly face—the Web—possess great potential for enhancing our fundraising efforts and increasing our results.

Have we raised money through the use of the Web? Have we built our constituency? The short answer is yes, but not perhaps as our readers might initially think. As many start-up companies have found, the Internet is not a magical money machine. Whether your business is hot sauce, secret-recipe fudge, or charitable undertakings, the Web will not do your work for you.

Having a Web site is very much like having a phone number. People won't "call" unless you give them a good reason to do so. And they won't give you money just because you are wired. Money *does* flow over the wires. Not just millions of dollars, and not just billions—but trillions. Very little of that flow travels over the Internet at present. Most of it travels between companies, banks, and countries over secure private wires. This will change. We are at the beginning of a massive new commercial flow to the Internet. As personal banking, personal shopping, corporate purchasing, and entertainment all move to the Internet, so will charitable giving.

We feel that libraries, universities, and other wired institutions will be among the first to benefit from this movement of personal commerce to the Internet. In very short order, almost every nonprofit institution will find the Web to be a useful venue for fundraising. Therefore, the purpose of this book is to help development officers, library administrators, and others to think about the fundraising potential of the Internet. To think about the potential—and then to act.

The companion "Web-enabled" CD is both a fruit of our experimentation and an extension of our mission: to give fundraisers a wealth of tips, tools, ideas, and signposts for getting started—or for taking current Web work in new and promising directions. Pop it into the CD-ROM drive of any Web-connected machine, and you will have direct access to the many resources that we have discovered and/or created for use by our colleagues.

The question of whether to focus this book on libraries or on the larger community of nonprofit institutions was the topic of much debate between us and our editors. In the end the editors won—as they usually do, and usually with good result. Therefore we will focus on what we know best: library fundraising. Libraries have become path-breakers on the digital frontier, and so have library fundraisers. The results of our experimentation will consequently be of value to everyone who works in the development arena.

There is a humorous saying about new ventures in the digital age: "In the old days, the sequence was 'Ready, aim, fire.' Now the order is 'Ready, fire, aim!'" In the past several years we at Penn* have done quite a bit of ready, fire, aim. That is to say, we have put projects "up" and waited to see how they would work. If they worked, we kept expanding the concept. If they didn't, we tried something else. We hope that this book will help other libraries, and other wired institutions, to have more "hits" than "misses." But don't worry, Web-based fundraising is not yet a science, nor is it an art. There is still time to have some fun.

* The University of Pennsylvania is a private institution located in Philadelphia, and is also known as "Penn." Pennsylvania State University, which is located in State College, Pennsylvania, is known as "Penn State."

PART I

Gifts on the Web

1

Fundraising and Friend-Raising

The biggest fundraising problem libraries face is that of being taken for granted. It is assumed that they will be available, well stocked, and ready to serve on a weeklong, year-round, basis—and without a direct charge to their customers. As the cast in the 1920s musical *Good News* might have sung: "The library belongs to everyone—the best things in life are free!"

Because most libraries are heavily subsidized, either through taxes or, in the case of universities, through tuition, there has been a slow acceptance of the need for fundraising on their behalf. In recent years, however, the public has come to understand that private charitable giving can be an important factor in the survival and enhancement of library services.

More and more libraries have undertaken fundraising programs, and these initiatives have proven to be increasingly fruitful. And why should they not? After all, the social and educational function of libraries is deeply engrained in the American psyche.

Libraries have a number of fundraising advantages. First, there is the accurate perception that libraries "belong to everybody," young and old, rich and poor, native and immigrant, scholar and amateur. Even at a private university such as ours, or at Princeton, or at UCLA, the determined seeker is usually admitted free or for a modest day-use fee.

Second, the library provides an easy link to any part of the university or the community. Whatever your interest, be it stamp collecting, business information, or philology, the library and the wider library network can usually meet your need. Conversely, library development officers can work with almost any interest as they seek to raise money. Do you love your pets? How about establishing a book fund for purchases of magazines and monographs on animal care? Are you an amateur genealogist? Perhaps you would like to create a family history center at your library.

Third, libraries and their collections provide some of the best opportunities for lasting memorials. Book plates, named book funds, wall plaques, named rooms, and named libraries are all wonderful ways to remember a loved one—or to be remembered.

Fourth, libraries are perceived as safe, warm, service-oriented, non-controversial, and they partake in the "romance of the book." Donors can feel that their gifts are associating them with something of broad and lasting value—as, indeed, they are!

Fifth, in the digital age, libraries have become electronic pioneers. As they lead the way into the twenty-first century, wired libraries can justly be seen as exciting and on the cutting edge. This opens up a whole new constituency for fundraising: technophiles, in addition to the traditional bibliophiles.

Sixth, libraries have a significant return for the investment. Often a gift of as little as $25 can buy a book. And endowed book funds, which last in perpetuity, can be started for $10,000 at many libraries.

Traditional Fundraising

It is a sad fact that in this less civic-minded era, some libraries have had to raise funds to *preserve* or *reinstate* services, such as Saturday hours or serial purchases. Most libraries, however, are attempting to raise "enhancement" dollars. That is to say, we raise funds for new projects, new purchases, and extra services, rather than for core services.

This "marginal" fundraising is much easier than core fundraising. After all, you are asking for funds to do something new, perhaps even unique. This is usually a much more attractive "sell" than paying the electricity bill.

Even if some library fundraising is for core services, the pattern of traditional library fundraising is fairly consistent. It is composed of five elements: membership and annual giving, corporate and foundation solicitation, benefits and drives; collections gifts, and individual major gift solicitation.

Web-based fundraising is not a substitute for any of these traditional activities. Rather, it can function as an enhancement in all of these areas, just as it can enhance your outreach and public relations efforts.

If your library does not have a fundraising program, we cannot recommend starting off with a heavy investment of time and money in creating a fundraising Web site. Keep in mind that "people give money to people" and your major efforts should be people oriented, not computer oriented.

At our library, we already had in place a Friends of the Library organization and a modest annual giving program. We already had a major gifts program, a foundation program, and a planned giving program. We already had brochures, fliers, and a Friends newsletter. We had years of planning special events and had undertaken more than one successful special project drive. We also had a tradition of substantial gifts of collections. In addition to all this, we were blessed with a very strong volunteer advisory group, called the Library Board of Overseers (the name taken from the English eleemosynary tradition, not from the Plantation South).

The focus of fundraising for the Penn Library has been on endowment-building and physical improvements—so-called "capital" fundraising. For the past five years, we have been able to raise over $2 million per year, and in the future we hope to raise more. Our annual giving numbers have been much more modest, running at $30,000 per year. Other libraries have placed a much greater emphasis on annual giving. The University of Illinois and the University of New Mexico, for example, have each raised over $500,000 per year in unrestricted annual funds.

Money like this does not get raised without effort. Such results come about because of full-time staffing and energetic fundraising programs, not because someone has a P.O. box or a Web address to which checks can be sent.

This book will not attempt to cover the basics of library fundraising. That task has been ably covered in *Becoming a Fundraiser: The Principles and Practice of Library Development,* by Victoria Steele and Stephen D. Elder (American Library Association, 1992), and *Friends of the Library Sourcebook,* Third Edition, by Sandy Dolnick (ALA, 1996). We can recommend both of these volumes for the beginning fundraiser or library administrator, as well as for those who want to consider enhancing or augmenting their traditional fundraising efforts.

Web-Enhanced Fundraising

We contend that libraries should be moving rapidly toward a Web-centered strategy for fundraising and friend-raising. Yes, you must pay attention to building your fundraising infrastructure; however, as the Internet plays a greater and greater role in what libraries are all about and how people use them, so will it come to shape your methods for communication with Friends and donor prospects.

We believe that most nonprofit organizations should consider moving toward a "Web-centric" communications model. The simple fact is that the Internet is going to revolutionize everything we do. Institutions that lag behind will lose customers, lose community support, and lose money.

Granted, "*people* raise money from people." Not Web pages, not displays, not plaques, not paperweights with your logo embedded in them. Even so, development officers and public relations officers who ignore the Web will do so at their personal peril. They will be like the job applicant who came to our office one day to interview for a grant writer position. We asked what word-processing package she used. "Why, none," she replied, "I can't use a computer at all." How, we asked, did she expect to produce foundation proposals? "I will write them on legal paper and hand them to a secretary," she responded. Since we didn't have a secretary, and every other candidate had word-processing skills, she didn't get the job!*

In thinking about a Web-centric office, imagine that you have been transported back in time ninety years. A bright young whippersnapper has just come to your office and wants to sell you a new device. He tells you that this device is going to radically change the way you handle public inquiries. It is going to change the way you stay in contact with your constituents. It is going to dramatically affect how you gather information and work with colleagues. One day you'll even use it to raise money for your organization.

It's called a telephone.

If you can imagine what it must have been like to ponder this new device in the early 1900s, then you may have an inkling of the magnitude of the change we are facing now.

The Internet is more than just an "update" on the phone. It combines the dynamic features of mail, of publishing, of radio, of television; it has the immediacy of a face-to-face encounter, and the excitement of a video game. Some people are comparing the advent of the Internet to the invention of the printing press, and they are predicting societal changes as far-reaching—yet in a much shorter span of time.

Making a Difference

It is already obvious that the Internet has major changes in store for those of us in the communications business. Here are some of the reasons it will make a difference in fundraising and friend-raising:

* We are happy to report that we ran into this woman two years later. She had learned word processing and was happily employed as a grant writer.

- Your library can create a new and exciting public "face" that can be changed and improved easily and can be accessible to a vast audience.
- You can almost instantaneously publish and make available any document to a global audience.
- You can alter and revise your communications in a matter of hours, even minutes.
- If you have unique information assets, they can be made directly available to your constituents, subscribers, or members—and possibly generate a revenue stream.
- You have all the benefits of interactivity: constituents can respond, ask questions, make reservations, *and send you money.*
- You can create communications matrixes for your volunteers and your constituents, so that they not only interact with you, they can interact with each other.
- You can publicize your events in new and exciting ways, building in interactivity so that your event site becomes an "event" in its own right.
- You can have "broadcast" ability, either through e-mail, or through newer "broadcast" capabilities such as those demonstrated by point-cast (*http://www.pointcast.com*) and the new Netscape and Microsoft browsers.
- You can undertake creative forms of donor recognition, as outlined in chapter 2.
- You can extend the power of the Web through related publications, such as brochures, personalized proposals, and "electronic brochures" on CD-ROM discs (see chapter 10).

Make no mistake: the Internet has made libraries very hot. It has even made them "cool"—a term that has transcended its trendiness and moved from cliche to classic. Why? Because *libraries can deliver a real product over the Internet.*

Libraries have information, and lots of it. This information can be accessed and delivered through the Internet. Can General Motors deliver its product over the Internet? No. Can McDonalds?

There are those who suggest that libraries will be made obsolete by the Internet and the digitization of information. To the contrary, libraries have taken on a new life and a new cachet. The range of possibilities provided by the Internet—for libraries working collectively or individually—is absolutely wonderful.

To repeat ourselves: the library has a great storefront location in cyberspace. Each and every day, libraries large and small attract customers through their online services—and these customers come back again and again. Whether it be the local public library, the high school library, or the Harvard library, the Internet provides new challenges and new opportunities for service.

In the chapters that follow, we will attempt to share some of what we have learned through our three years of experimentation with the Web. We will show how creative use of the Internet has enhanced our major gift fundraising and how it can be used to attract and hold new constituents. We will suggest new possibilities for direct online gifts and give some ideas for "positioning" your library in cyberspace. We will also share some start-up tips and tricks, as well as practical advice. Finally, we will cite Web resources by address so that our readers can explore for themselves, and we have included a Web-enabled disc that makes it very easy to find these resources with a simple mouse-click.

Where useful, we will bring in examples from other nonprofit sites, such as the Red Cross. The aim of these chapters will be to stimulate the thinking of our readers and to provide tools for getting started.

Fair enough? If this were a Web page, we would say "click here for more." But in a book, one simply turns the page.

2

Major Gifts

One day a very significant amount of money will be donated to libraries and other nonprofit institutions through direct transfer via the Internet. But that day may be quite a few years off. At present, we believe that the Web is currently most useful in soliciting and acknowledging major gifts, and in this chapter we will share our reasoning and our experience.

We contend that if your library or nonprofit organization has a major gifts program, then your Web-building should focus on this program first and foremost. Why? Because "that's where the money is" and that's where your Internet investment will begin to pay off.

If your institution does not have a major gifts program, you should consider starting one. Consider these two tales:

Tale the first

At the Penn Library, we conducted a minicampaign to raise $300,000 to create a Music Study Center in honor of Marian Anderson. A native Philadelphian, she decided to donate her personal papers and memorabilia to our library so that these materials would be available for scholarly research.

We decided to take advantage of a generous offer by the Philadelphia Orchestra to use their annual Martin Luther King Concert as a benefit fundraiser. The idea was simple: the orchestra would make seats available to us at a discount, and we would sell them at regular price. We could sell as many tickets as we could handle.

Knowing that this would be an attractive idea on campus, we organized a significant benefit effort. We enlisted the aid of numerous student and fraternal organizations. We involved alumni groups. We reached out to local organizations. We printed fliers and special invitations and got advance stories in the campus media. We set up a patron's level ticket which included a pre-concert dinner at a downtown restaurant. We got a local jazz club to host a jazz party after the concert, to which our ticket-buyers were admitted free.

After three months of increasing intensity, the day of the concert came. We were pleased that we had sold three hundred tickets at various price levels, and that we had a patrons dinner of about twenty VIPs. The concert was great; the jazz party was fun. Everyone had a wonderful time.

Total net: $6,000

Tale the second

The library had a donor who had created a book fund in honor of his father with a gift of $20,000. This gift had been made as a pledge, payable over four years at $5,000 per year. After the last payment, the development office had a report drawn up on the purchases made through the fund and mailed it to the donor. Adam followed up with a call to thank the donor for his generosity and to see if he had any questions about the fund and its purchases.

"No, everything's just fine. I'm happy to see what the fund is acquiring. You know, I think I'll just keep giving $5,000 for several more years until I bring the fund to $50,000." Adam thanked him warmly and rang off.

Total net: $30,000

Every fundraiser who has been around the block a few times can tell a similar tale. Major fundraising happens when you can find major donors. The ratio of time and energy spent to results gained is usually so dramatic that one wonders why so many fundraisers spend so much of their time on special events and small-gift appeals.

The answer is (or should be) that special events and annual/membership appeals are constituency-building activities. Libraries need their Friends, public radio needs its members—not just as a pool for future fundraising, but as a base of institutional support. Our Marian Anderson Orchestra Event made a lot of new friends for the library. It also enhanced the image of the library among students and staff on campus, and it added to Penn's reputation off campus. Many people realized for the first time that an important part of Marian Anderson's legacy was being preserved at the Penn Library.

These factors made the event worthwhile. Nevertheless, in our successful drive to meet the Anderson Goal ($300,000) we raised only $75,000 from gifts of $5,000 and under, and the remaining $225,000 came from five major donors. Moral: Major donor work pays off.

Hence another truism of fundraising: once you have a full-fledged development program up and running, 80 percent of your gifts will come from 20 percent of your donors. This will be particularly true if your library is engaged in capital fundraising, that is, for large-scale renovation, building, or endowment purposes.

The related notion that goes along with this truism is that development staff should be spending 80 percent of their time focusing on the 20 percent of prospects who have high gift potential. This rarely happens, particularly in one-person shops, but it is a very important yardstick to keep in mind.

Recognition As Fundraising

So what does this have to do with the Web? Plenty.

Your development Web site can be a wonderful place to recognize major donors to your institution. It can also be a wonderful way to involve major donors and major prospects with your institution in new and compelling ways. Donor recognition can lead to second-time gifts and inspire new first-time gifts.

Take a hypothetical example: David Zinc collects rare books. He is a member of your Friends of the Library and enjoys turning out for lectures and exhibition openings. You hope that he will eventually donate his books to the Library and endow a fund to purchase additional rare books and manuscripts.

Standard library approach: your special collections director asks Mr. Zinc if he would be willing to loan some of his books for an exhibition. He agrees. This leads to many warm conversations as books are reviewed for the show. All of this leads to a nice opening reception where Friends and friends appear, where much fuss is made over Mr. Zinc, and a souvenir catalog or program is distributed.

Somewhere in the process of all this, a discussion occurs with regard to a possible gift of the collection and the creation of a named endowed fund to support the collection. Thousands of wonderful gifts have come to libraries and museums in just this way.

Wired library approach: All of the above, plus the following. The librarian or development director tells Mr. Zinc that the library would like to put the exhibition online. A meeting is held in a location where a networked computer is available. They show him how other exhibitions have been placed on the Net. They show how the donor is recognized. They show how memorial recognition is done online. Might Mr. Zinc like to dedicate the online show to the memory of his wife? Might he have a picture of the couple available that could be put up on the dedication page?

Three months go by. The "real" exhibition has to come down. But the virtual exhibition stays on. Comments have been coming in from Internet visitors from as far away as Japan. These comments are shared with Mr. Zinc, who is slightly amazed that midwestern professors and Italian undergraduates have visited his site. Wouldn't it be wonderful to enhance and augment the site? It can become a destination site for people who are interested in his field of concentration. Would Mr. Zinc like to help fund an expansion of the Zinc Digital Rare Book site?

Mr. Zinc is not only flattered, he is thoroughly engaged. He can see that the wired library can make his personal collection into a treasure for a worldwide audience. And that his wife's memory is being recognized in ways that she could never have imagined. Plus his children have become enthusiastically involved. They have been telling their friends to cruise to the Zinc site. You have made some valuable friends in the next generation of the family.

As this story illustrates, a presence on the Web allows for interesting new ways in which to engage a prospective donor's interest. The Web is still so visual that it can capture the attention of almost anyone. We well recall a committee meeting that included a major donor whose spouse was visiting another building on campus. When she returned, the meeting was still in progress, and so we showed her the new site we had created with her husband's picture accompanying some beautiful illustrations from his collection. "Look, you're on the Web!" she exclaimed when he came out of the meeting, and pulled him over to see the screen.

A nice aspect of a Web site is that it is portable. If your donor is "wired," you can view the site on her machine. If not, she can come in to your headquarters and see the site on your screen. Furthermore, you can load exemplary sites on your laptop and take it with you anywhere. You can set it on the coffee table of a donor couple and take them on a tour. We have done it in Delaware. You can take it into the office of a busy executive and capture his full attention for fifteen minutes. We have done that in southern California. You can even sit at a dinner table with five members of an extended donor family and pass the laptop around while each explores your pages and points out things to the others. We did that in western Pennsylvania.

The key concept here is "engagement." The more that an engaged, collaborative relationship exists between you and your donor, the more likely that you will receive continued and committed support. Particularly for libraries, where colorless brass plaques can abound and where rare materials can seem to be locked away from the public, the Web adds a whole new dimension of visibility and access. Global visibility, worldwide access! And your donor gets to go along for the ride.

Electronic Plaquing

The Web allows for new forms of recognition, and new ways to honor or memorialize a special friend or benefactor. There isn't a term for this yet, but we have been calling it electronic recognition, or sometimes "cyber-plaquing."

For a fascinating look at the possibilities of cyber-plaquing, consider our Class of '43/Murphy Memorial site.

Fred Murphy entered Penn as a freshman in 1939. He should have graduated with his friends in 1943 but by then he was a medic with the Army's 65th Infantry Division. Murphy left college in the middle of his freshman year, went home, got married, and joined the Army.

On March 18, 1945, his regiment was in the midst of a battle at the Siegfried Line in Germany—all part of the Allied push toward the Rhine. Land mines were everywhere, and a number of soldiers had been maimed or killed. Murphy, unarmed, stayed on the battlefield and tended the wounded despite being repeatedly wounded himself. While aiding others, he crawled across a mine and was killed.

Frederick C. Murphy was awarded the Congressional Medal of Honor for his "indomitable courage and unquestionable spirit of self-sacrifice and supreme devotion to duty." His daughter, Susan, born two months after he died, accepted the honor on his behalf.

The class of 1943, of which Murphy would have been a part, had not realized that they had a hero in their ranks. Only recently did the class leadership become aware of this story, and they approached the library to see if Murphy could be honored in some way. The class had just completed a reunion drive to build a new circulation area at the library, and they asked about the placement of a memorial plaque.

Of course, we said. The '43 Circulation Area was due to be completed in 1998. But in addition, what about also doing something on the Web?

Thus began a process of gathering information and images, aided by the class president, Jack Lawler. By January 1997, we were able to mount a substantial site in Murphy's honor.

The '43 site contains pictures of the class at its 1993 reunion and a drawing of the space that it is dedicating. The site also contains exten-

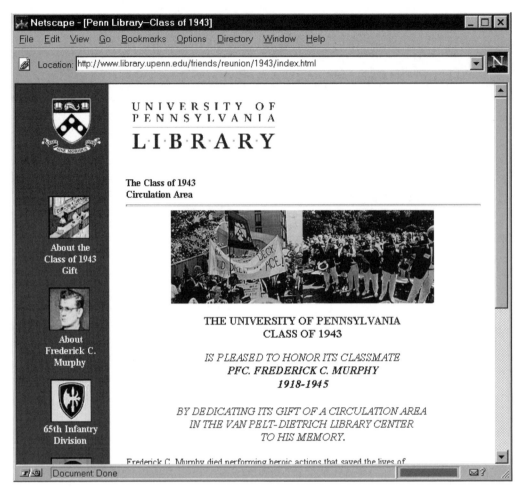

sive information about Murphy. In addition to his portrait, there are links to another of our pages which describes his acts of heroism, an Internet link to the Web pages of a federal building named in his honor in Massachusetts, links to a page we created on his Division (which honored him at its 50th reunion in 1994), an Internet link to a Medal of Honor information site, and links to a Penn Library page containing a moving personal essay by Murphy's grandson.

Before the site was formally placed on the library's "Friends and Benefactors" pages, we previewed the site with the class leadership. The pages were downloaded to a laptop and linked to a projector. It may have been the first time many of them had seen this material. We also printed out the pages from the site and presented them to each member in a Penn folder.

We are also considering placing the site on a floppy disk that can be viewed through a Web browser (see chapter 10) or through its own mini-browser. These disks could be mailed to members of the class, to Murphy's family, and possibly to veterans of the 65th Infantry Division.

Prior to the advent of the Web, it would have been impossible to create anything like the '43/Murphy site, short of producing a small book. But even a small book would not be able to contain live links to other evolving sites, which themselves contain links to other sites.

Here are some other examples of what can be done:

- The Richard III Society created a memorial page for member Judy R. Weinsoft, who, despite undergoing chemotherapy for breast cancer, continued to prepare, and delivered, a significant lecture at the 1993 Oregon Shakespeare Festival. Judy created a Library Endowment Fund for the Society through bequest. A moving tribute to Judy is contained on the site, along with a picture, the full text of the lecture, and an invitation to add to the fund in Judy's memory. (*http://www.r3.org/weinsoft.html*)

- Alex G. Spanos, owner of the San Diego Chargers, donated $1 million to the American Red Cross to aid the victims of floods in California. His donation was recognized at some length as a special article in their "News" area. Spanos was quoted as saying "I hope my contribution will serve as an inspiration to others to make a difference in the lives of these flood victims by making a donation today to the Red Cross." At the bottom of the page was donation information, including a clickable link to make an online credit card donation. (*http://www.redcross.org/news/disaster/97/01-10-97a.html*)

- When the Safra Business Research Center was opened at Penn's Lippincott Business Library, the opening festivities were captured with a digital camera, and snapshots of the new space were put on a "Grand Opening" Web site. The site included pictures of Safra family members touring with the library director and the Wharton School dean. (*http://www.library.upenn.edu/friends/safra/index.html*)

- Science fiction writer Piers Anthony donated his manuscripts and papers to the library at the University of South Florida Tampa campus. A few years later he and his wife donated $200,000 to the Library's oral history program. A special recognition page was created, with a picture of the couple, a tribute, and a link to extensive information about the Piers Anthony Collection. (*http://www.lib.usf.edu/development/piers.html*) USF Library also made a deal with the Tampa Bay Mutiny professional soccer team for "USF Night" at the stadium, with $3.00 of every ticket going to the library. The event was publicized on several Web pages. (*http://www.lib.usf.edu/development/mutiny.html*)

- The Metropolitan Museum of Art received support for its Winslow Homer exhibition from GTE. At the beginning of the online exhibition page, the corporation is thanked, its chairman is quoted as saying "Our support of the arts and education reflects our desire to enhance the quality of life in our society," and four separate links that go directly to the GTE home page are given. (*http://www.metmuseum.org/htmlfile/homer/homer.html*)

The possibilities in electronic plaquing are limited only by one's imagination, by the wishes of the donor, and by the self-imposed restraints of the institution. Would the donor like to be pictured with his favorite hunting dog? It can be done. Could a spoken message from the donor be included? Certainly. How about a video clip of the recognition dinner or the library director saying laudatory things at the ribbon cutting? Why not?

We believe that *good stewardship is good fundraising*. Although churches use "stewardship" as a euphemism for donations, to a fundraising professional stewardship means those activities that acknowledge and recognize a donor and that report on the use of the gift. A well-thanked and well-recognized donor is an inspiration to other prospective supporters. Furthermore, a happy donor is an excellent prospect for a second gift, and a third—as every major gift officer can attest.

Therefore, we recommend that donor recognition be one of the *first* things that any nonprofit does with its Web site, rather than something that is attempted after your "case" is fully online. Take it from us, you will always be adding to and amending your "case" pages. Don't wait to be finished before doing some attractive donor recognition.

(For additional donor recognition sites—and insights—see the "Cool Sites" section of our companion CD.)

Results

A number of people have asked us whether we can trace actual new gifts to the electronic recognition fundraising strategy. We have been doing this for only three years, but the short answer is yes. Without violating any confidences, we can share that as we write one donor family has made a second major gift and is considering two more. Another donor has begun adding regularly to our special purchase fund. Another increased his six-figure contribution by an additional 50 percent. Still another is contemplating a multimillion dollar gift, nurtured by personal visits as well as virtual ones. The Web was not the sole motivator in any of these cases, but it helped considerably in deepening and extending our relationships, and in enhancing our reputation as a cutting-edge institution.

Several donors have extended themselves greatly, digging up old photos or having special ones taken. Others have spent hours combing through their site and other sites and sending us corrections. Many more have "told their friends" about our work, and in some cases have asked us to send notices of their URL (Web address) to mailing lists that they supply.

Liz Sismilich, director of development at USF Tampa, says that corporate and foundation donors "have responded very well" to Web recognition. The Tampa Bay Mutiny soccer team was eager to work with the school, having before them the prospect of reaching a student/alumni/staff audience of almost 200,000 people. As for the practice of creating links to corporate pages from the Web recognition site: "they love it."

The Mix: Ways of Saying Thanks

There is another fundraising saw that goes like this: *A donor can never be thanked too often, or by too many people.*

People sometimes ask us if we think that Web recognition can substitute for print and plaque recognition. The short answer is no. Our contention is that Web recognition should be in addition to other forms of stewardship.

The Penn Library recently received a spectacular gift for the complete renovation of our information processing center (cataloging and acquisitions), as well as for the creation of an electronic training classroom. We have so far thanked the donor couple in the following ways:

1. Many phone calls, letters, and personal visits to say "thanks."

2. Special mention by the university provost at a symposium that the donor couple attended, and a round of applause.

3. A special event at the sites, showing them off in mid-construction, which involved speeches, souvenir hard hats, and free food and drink. Lovely color photos from this event were sent to the donors.

4. A nicely designed Web site that has the donors' picture, a quote from the alumni half of the couple, an artist's conception of the spaces, a description of the spaces and what they will accomplish, a link to the new donor-named Directorship of Information Processing, with a picture and grateful quote from the recipient; a link to the Information Processing Center site (now renamed for the donor) with tons of library information, including reviews of new books.

5. A related press release that the donor reviewed and approved.

6. A thank-you lunch in New York for friends, family, and colleagues of the donor. Each person received a packet containing printed pages from the Web site. (And, by the way, additional gifts came in from this group, in honor of the donors.)

7. A gala ribbon-cutting dedication event on Alumni Day, with other donors in attendance, and the president expressing her gratitude on behalf of the entire university community.

8. An extensive article, with pictures, and based on personal interviews, in our *Planned Giving Newsletter,* which will go out to thousands of alumni.

9. Two handsome plaques, with language approved by the donors, as well as their name being etched in glass at the entrance to both facilities.

And perhaps other things that we dream up along the way.

Note that the Web site was just one of the things we did by way of saying thanks. But also note that a Web site is a "living" entity that can still evolve and that will continue to be shared with the donor, and other prospective donors, as the years go by.

Tips and Ideas

This is a new area. One in which we shall each have an opportunity to be creative and to learn from one another. Here are a few tips and a few ideas that we can add to the mix:

- Get a "volunteer" for your first recognition page. Every NPO (non-profit organization) needs an example of a donor recognition page to show to and inspire other potential donors. An excellent "volunteer" might be a historic figure who helped found or build your institution, such as the University of Virginia's Thomas Jefferson. Or someone who made an important bequest (and whose family is in agreement). San Diego State University persuaded a faculty member who had donated an important collection to be their first Web "role model." At Penn we put up pages for a reunion class, a bequest from a much-loved dean, and a gift from a member of our board—all at about the same time.

- Make sure to obtain the donor's approval before putting her name on a Web site. So far, only one donor has asked to remain anonymous, but all donors should be given that option.

- The idea of approval should probably extend to "Honor Roll" lists; for example, lists of reunion donors. Even though these donors may have been given the option to remain anonymous on the printed Honor Roll, that decision should not be assumed to transfer to the online Honor Roll unless it was made explicit during the gift process.

- Keep copyright in mind. If a wonderful picture of your donor appears in the local newspaper, do not scan and post that picture without permission from the newspaper and/or the photographer.

- Copyright issues can also abound with regard to your donor's collection of books or art. If any of this material was created in the twentieth century, it is wise to check on "rights" before putting images on your Web page.

- Consider interviewing the donor especially for the Web site. Donor sites should be ones in which you can experiment. If you are not ready to put audio or video on your main page, why not try something with a donor page? Usually such pages are not intended primarily to provide public service, so there should be less worry if some visitors can't access everything there due to a missing "plug-in."

- Remember that you can print pages once you create them. Donors who do not have Web-browsing computers may still be pleased to have color prints of their Web site. These pages can be bound in a custom donor book for keeping on one's shelf or coffee table. Even black-and-white printouts of Web sites look attractive.

- Why not print out and frame the main page of your donors' site and give it to them as a gift?

- In later chapters (chapters 10 and 11) we will discuss the exciting possibilities presented by "Web-enabled" CDs and floppy disks. Basically, these allow you to download Web sites to disks, which can then be viewed at "high bandwidth" speed. These disks present many interesting possibilities for outreach and recognition. For instance, we created an "Introduction" to an online exhibition, using a floppy disk that contained all of the main pages of the exhibit, plus several color images. The disk could be viewed with or without an Internet connection, and with or without a browser. We mailed it to two hundred close friends of the collector.

We trust this chapter will have stimulated the imaginations of our readers, and look forward to seeing what each of you will create in the years ahead! Remember: don't be afraid to spend time on this. The payoff may well be worth every minute.

3

Money on
the Net

Money will be made via the Internet. Just how much money—and how soon—is subject to intense speculation. Will Internet commerce total $10 billion in three years, or $800 billion in five? Either way, we are talking about some serious transfers, and some of those transfers will be in the form of charitable donations.

We have already demonstrated that the Internet can be used to provide a unique form of donor recognition and thus to motivate major gifts. We will also show in chapters 4 and 5 that it can gain you new friends and convey your "story."

But can the Internet become a tool for direct contributions to your institution? Yes it can.

Online Pledges

One day we will hear the news about Caleb Crabtree's online pledge of $5 million to the Hummingbird Society. You know Caleb. He lives in a shack, wears old clothes, never talks to his neighbors, and apparently doesn't have a dime. Turns out he spends all his time cruising the Internet, and the Hummingbird home page caught his eye. Caleb was moved by the story of the loss of hummingbird habitat in the rain forest. When the "pledge now" icon appeared at the bottom of the page, he clicked and entered $5 million, plus his name and phone number.

Of course, anyone can enter any amount in an online pledge form, and the staff of the Hummingbird Society figured it was a joke. Someone called anyway, and—miracle of miracles—good-hearted Caleb has it all buried in a Charles Schwab account. He got it by turning in soda cans for the deposit money, and then played the market for fifteen years. Caleb is a stock-market genius, and the Hummingbird Society has struck it rich.*

All it takes is one story like this to set everyone scrambling for on-line megapledges. We rather doubt that gifts of this size will come from online pledge forms, any more than $5 million gifts appear regularly in response envelopes to your annual appeals.

When it comes to major gifts, and especially major-major gifts, "people give money to people," and the bigger the gift, the more direct personal involvement will be required. You can't just put a few pictures on the Web, add some compelling text, and expect the big bucks to roll in— any more than you would let a few brochures carry your entire fundraising burden.

Nevertheless, it would be foolish *not* to set up an online pledging site on your home page. The development people at Wake Forest decided to try such an approach, and were pleasantly surprised to find that several pledges were registered. One was for $2,500. Not $5 million, but not bad!

Once you have received an online pledge, treat it as you would a phone pledge. Ask the donor to confirm it in writing, with a signature. Or send a standard pledge form, if your institution has created one. Better yet, arrange a visit to thank the donor, and take the form with you!

There is ample proof that signed pledges have legal standing, and institutions have won court cases in which the donor died and the heirs challenged the pledge. But you wouldn't want to show up in court with an e-mail printout as your only proof of intent!

Use of Credit or Debit Cards Online

Credit and debit cards may provide a very substantial source of donations via the Internet. Many institutions are already geared up to receive credit card payments and gifts by mail or by phone, and it would seem a short walk to establish an Internet mechanism for accepting contributions.

As people become accustomed to using credit cards online to buy football tickets, T-shirts, and toasters, they will be more likely to make an "impulse" gift (or a predetermined gift) at your site. Such gifts will probably be in the $25 to $250 range, but you'll take a few hundred of those, won't you? The Red Cross thinks this is a distinct possibility and

---

*After posting this chapter in draft form online, we discovered that there really is a Hummingbird Society, and they really have a Web page: *www.hummingbird.org*. Their president sent us an e-mail saying that they would be happy to hear from Caleb Crabtree, or any would-be Calebs!

has established a straightforward mechanism for making online credit card donations. (See chapter 4.)

Presently there is a strong resistance to using the Internet for credit card transactions. The ostensible reason is security. Potential customers (read "donors") are concerned that their credit or debit card numbers will be hijacked in cyberspace. Providers (read "your nonprofit") are concerned about wholesale theft and massive losses. As a consequence, heroic efforts are being made to create "secure" transactions over the Internet, so that the public can be assured that all is safe, and providers can manage their risk.

Companies like Microsoft and Netscape have rushed to create secure systems for online commercial transactions, hoping that a flood of money will run through their pipeline. Yet just when the consumer thinks that it's safe to go into the water, the press gleefully reports the cracking of someone's security system, and pundits proclaim that the vaunted new era of cybercommerce may never come.

This is silly. Take out the credit card brochure you received when you first signed up—you know, the brochure with the small print. You will find a sentence that reads something like this: "In the event that this card is lost or stolen, customer's liability shall not exceed $50."

A fifty-dollar hit is not exactly a cause for panic. Yet the press, and the public, act as though a cyberswipe of your credit card number is akin to having hurricane Andrew pass through your neighborhood.

Every year millions of people gleefully order billions of dollars of merchandise over the phone. They hand their credit cards to their kids. They leave them lying on counters. They sign their names to millions of slips of paper that carry their number and their expiration date, and casually drop their receipts in the wastebasket.

The *real* reason that people have not started using the Internet in massive numbers for commercial transactions is that *it is a new activity and it involves money.* Remember the first time you used an automated teller machine? Or the first time you proffered your debit card at the supermarket? It takes a while for people to get comfortable with new mechanisms for commerce; in fact, it takes a while for people to adjust to *any* new technology. And in fact, as we go to press, the industry is paving the way for greater acceptance of Internet-based transactions with TV commercials designed to reassure consumers that these transactions are, in fact, as safe as any other kind of transaction.

What To Do Now

Remembering that the quick brown fox jumps over the proverbial dog, we would advise development directors to start preparing for the day when online giving becomes a reality. Initiate discussions with your business manager now. Find out what he or she knows about handling on-line transactions. Encourage him or her to explore options. If you can find another institution that is ahead of yours in this new area, find out who the in-house expert is, give that person a call, and put your key player in touch with their key player.

Most nonprofits undertake very little risk in getting involved with online gifts. Fraudulent gifts would be a nuisance, but hardly a disaster. Having a hacker steal credit card numbers from your cache would be embarrassing and could harm donor relations—so clearly great pains should be taken to prevent such theft. Yet your institution will not be set-ting itself up as a bank or a credit card issuer, so the actual financial risk would seem quite limited.

Don't wait for online credit card transactions to be deemed "safe" by *Newsweek* or the Mellon Bank before setting up your Web site. If you or your administration are not comfortable accepting such gifts, you should still go ahead and get your Web site up and running. There are plenty of good reasons to have your site up right now, and when you are ready to accept online gifts, you will be able to add that component almost instantaneously.

One thing you can do is *handle a little cybercash.* If you haven't used a card or a digital cash account online, sign up for such a service and try it out. Go ahead, buy a book, buy a CD. Buy something. Watch your own emotions as you engage in this new activity. This will help you educate others and will free up your imagination.

The other thing that you should do is to *start dreaming.* Imagine that your prospective donors could hand you money with the click of a mouse button. What clever inducements could you create for online giving? Can't think of any? We have a few imaginative ideas coming right up.

Digital Cash

One of the most difficult concepts to grasp in the new world of cyber-commerce is the notion of "digital cash."

Digital cash is different from using a credit or debit card online, the key difference being that digital cash is anonymous, just like real cash. If a clerk in a store hands you $3.25 in change, none of those dollars has the clerk's name on it, nor does the quarter. The money doesn't have the store's name on it. In fact, the store may have received the three dollar bills from three different customers, and *their* names aren't on the money either.

At its simplest, digital cash is just a unique electronic message—a message that says "I am worth [say] one dollar," or "I am worth five cents." In the not-too-distant future, we will send such electronic messages to each other, to stores, to our alma mater, to our favorite charity, as freely and confidently as we swap three bucks at the market for a gallon of milk.

After all, paper money is just a "message." In the United States, and in most countries, such printed messages are treated as though they have real value—and because they are treated that way, they do!

Here is how it might work. Aunt Millie wants to do a little cyber-shopping from her home in Moosehead, Montana. She cranks up the old computer and establishes a connection with her bank. She tells the bank (electronically) that she wants to withdraw $200 in digital cash. The bank's computer debits her checking or savings or credit card account and sends her $200 in encoded messages. Imagine these messages as each having a unique serial number, and further, imagine that they have the bank's code as the issuing agent. But *they don't have Aunt Millie's name on them;* they are simply in her possession.

She pockets the "cash" by storing it in the cashbox of her computer's money-management account. Now she is ready to shop.

Click, click, click, she visits the L.L. Bean store online. The Maine duck-hunting boots look nice and practical. She enters her size, her address, her phone. The screen asks if she wants to pay with cash, or credit, or through a direct transfer from her bank. She picks cash. That will be $89.83, the store says. She clicks up nine $10 messages from her cash-box and drags them to the store's cash register symbol. The store electronically validates the unique ID numbers of the digital cash units with its international fraud alert agency. L.L. Bean then sends Aunt Millie thirteen cents in change. The cash exchange has taken ten seconds. The boots will arrive tomorrow.

Click, click, click, Aunt Millie heads for her favorite soap opera home page. She wants to catch up on whether Brett told Cynthia about his skiing trip with Doreen. There is a charge of fifty cents to go to the plot summary pages. She pays it with a quick click and drag. It so happens that the writer for the show is online. Would she like to enter the script forum and pose some questions? Heck yes, it's only $2. More digital cash is exchanged. Aunt Millie gives that writer her two cents' (actually two dollars') worth: Brett should never have left his first wife, and further-more, Doreen is only pretending to care for his two teenage girls. And has the writer ever thought of getting Cynthia to wake up and smell the coffee? Yes, the writer has thought of that possibility, and she should stay tuned for some surprises on the show next week.

She copies her exchange with the writer to her sister in Akron. They both watch the show religiously. That $2.50 was well spent. Note that, unlike L.L. Bean, the soap opera home page didn't ask for her name, ad-dress, or phone number. It didn't link her payments with a preexisting account. It just took the cash. Happily.

Meanwhile, L.L. Bean has closed its books for the day. It has swept all of its cash transactions into a large cash deposit with its online bank. The soap home page has all of its books handled by an agency, and the digital cash is deposited within sixty seconds after the customer transfers it.

Aunt Millie now has $107.67 in her cashbox. She had noticed an advertisement for a new book about Prince Charles on the soap home page. Maybe she'll cruise to that site and read the first chapter—for free. If she likes it, she can order the book, or pay to read the next chapter online. The book has been self-published by the author, without the involvement of a publishing house. *Variety* says he made $350,000 last year, half of which was in digital cash.

Suspend for the moment your disbelief. People were pretty dubious about paper money when it was first issued! Yes, counterfeiting can occur. Yes, there will have to be mechanisms for "storing" your cash in a safe place in case your hard disk crashes. But rest assured, digital cash is coming, and it will reshape the marketplace. Media conglomerates will make money from it; mom-and-pop home pages will make money from it. Even Aunt Millie is thinking about writing a guide to Montana duck hunting and putting it online!

Fundraising with Digital Cash

So, how can your institution make money from digital cash?

The short answer is, nobody knows yet. Digital cash is being talked about; it is being experimented with, but it is still in the early stages of experimentation. Nevertheless, we can begin to imagine the possibilities now, and some of them will come true.

The key thing to keep in mind is that digital cash fundraising is at the opposite extreme from major gift fundraising. It will focus on gathering up many small gifts, perhaps as small as ten cents per donor, and in many cases these gifts will be anonymous.

Possibility A

Good Old Siwash U. has decided to adopt a mascot—after 150 years without one. After all, the football team has been doing well, and so has women's hockey. Yet people keep calling the teams the "Siwashers" and the students are fed up.

The Siwash Alumni Association announces a participatory contest. Should the university use an eagle for its mascot, or a bear? And what should the mascot be named? Alumni and other loyal fans are invited to vote by clicking over to the Alumni Association home page. Each vote costs fifty cents in digital cash, the proceeds to be used for the new athletics house. Would the loyal alum also like to suggest a name? For $2 a name can be submitted to the alumni judging panel; the winner gets season tickets for life.

Possibility B

The visitor to the St. Bartholomew's Hospital home page has many options to choose from. There is the prayer room, an ask-the-doctor section, a patient registry, a virtual tour of the planned new pediatrics wing, . . . and the Bingo game.

Click on Bingo and you will find that a new game starts every ten minutes. Each game costs a dollar, payable in digital cash. Prizes range from $50 (payable to you in digital cash) to the grand prize for the week of $1,000 (payable by check). Since the hospital has started online bingo, they have raised $400,000 toward their new wing. And that has been done in three months!

Possibility C

The Alice Paul Shelter for Battered Women is running out of funds. The demand for services has been high, and state funds for such programs have been reduced. The director sends out an urgent appeal on e-mail to the shelter's mailing list. Friends of the shelter are asked to click to the Alice Paul home page and give whatever they can, even twenty-five cents. An "Emergency" icon has been created, it leads to a pledging and gift site.

The shelter also persuades the local radio station to broadcast its appeal, and its URL, as a public service. The station also places an emergency appeal icon on *its* home page. By the end of the week, some 3,000 friends have made cash donations ranging from a quarter to $20; and several large pledges have come in from new sources. The crisis has been met, and overcome.

Possibility D

Imagine that the American Heart Association has a special relationship with game designer Sara Fernholt. Not only is she a large and regular contributor, but she has offered an exclusive on her new game, *Myhrvold's Secret.* Here is how the deal works. For two weeks, the Heart Association has exclusive preview rights to the new game. Web cruisers who travel to the Association's home page can play the game at ten cents a minute. Their usage will be metered as they play, and the cash will be automatically deducted every minute. Fans of Fernholt's previous hit, *Gates and Devices,* flock to the Heart Association's site. In fact, 300,000 people attempt to sign on in the first day, causing the Association's server to crash. That's OK, because the crash makes all the major papers the next morning. Meanwhile, Fernholt has allowed the game to be mounted on her supercomputer, and overflow is bounced from the Heart Association. The next day 420,000 people sign on, and the parade of dimes begins.

Having set out a variety of interesting possibilities, we are aware that a digital cash strategy that fits with libraries has not been produced. Here is one possibility: a donation box. The concept is very simple. Most of us have seen the Plexiglas donation boxes at the entrances to art and science museums. It would be easy to create a "donation box" icon on the library's home page, or to have it appear when you exit a session of searching. A freewill offering could be made by the grateful patron, using digital cash.

A more sophisticated version could look like this: a library might run a series of special appeals for needed items. Let's say the library needs $4,000 to purchase special computer equipment for the visually impaired. A special appeal icon could be mounted on the home page. When the patron clicks, she sees a picture of the equipment, reads a brief statement of the need, and is given an opportunity to make a cash donation on the spot. Further, there is a graph showing how much has been raised so far in the drive, and how much has been donated thus far today. When she makes her donation, she sees both graphs mark an increase automatically. The site also tells her that 324 people have donated so far, and after her gift the number goes to 325. And, by the way, would she like to enter the name of the high school she attended? Abington High School? Why, twenty-seven Abington graduates have donated so far. That's three more than Cheltenham High. Good going! Tell your friends.

New Technology at Work

In cruising through nonprofit cyberspace, we have come across some interesting examples of trolling for gifts online. Since new sites come up every day, we encourage our readers to try their own searches for creative fundraising ideas. Phrases that seem to work well in search engines are: "donate online," donate on-line," "online donation form," "online pledge," "on-line pledge," and "donate now."

Pledges   • Montana Public Television station KUSM is ready to accept online pledges at *http://visions.montana.edu/visions/ViewersLikeYou/*. For a pledge of $50, you can choose between a number of attractive premiums, including a Glenn Miller CD and a Lawrence Welk ball cap. Simply select your gift level and your premium, click "send," and the station will bill you for your pledge—or call you at your request.

- The University of Rhode Island will also take your pledge (*http://www.davis.uri.edu/*) and a pull-down menu allows you to direct your gift to the annual fund, parents' fund, capital campaign, or athletics.

- Benefice, a service provider for nonprofit organizations, has created a Web site called Benefice On-line, which allows viewers to make online pledges to over "2396 nonprofits in our system." Their site also allows visitors to learn more about individual organizations or to research causes by type (*http://www.benefice.com/html/pledge.cgi*).

- ReliefNet keeps a site of disaster and relief organizations and hosts a pledge page where you can make a direct commitment to any organization that they list (*http://www.reliefnet.org/pledge.html*). In a clever marketing ploy, they persuaded a number of music sites to appear online at "ReliefRock" (*http://www.reliefnet.org/reliefrock/rock.html*). Do you like "underground" music? The ReliefRock site will link you to a spot where you can download and listen to all 6:39 minutes of "Passion (and Fulfillment)," by Angel's Dream. On the way there you will see ReliefNet's "make a pledge" icon.

Credit Card Gifts

- The Nature Conservancy is well configured to allow for secure on-line credit card memberships (*http://www.tnc.org/*). Select "membership" from their attractive home page, and you are presented with the opportunity to use your American Express, MasterCard, Visa, or Discover card, and indicate whether you wish to join or renew at the $25 level on up to the $1,000 level. While you are visiting their site, you might just want to apply online for their own branded MasterCard. The card with the tree frog is pretty cute, and the otter card is adorable!

- The American Cancer Society encourages "Memorial or Honor Gift Donations" at their online credit-card site: *http://www.cancer.org/memform.html*. And, of course, the American Red Cross has a beautiful donor site, with plenty of giving options, at *http://www.redcross.org*.

Digital Cash

Many of us have already made an electronic cash gift—or at least have been given the opportunity to do so—at our local supermarket. While going through the checkout line, nestled among the copies of *TV Guide* and eyeglass repair kits, customers sometimes will find a packet of tear-off coupons that contain a bar code. In our region, the "Check Out Hunger" campaign has coupons for $1, $2, and $5. "Cashier will add amount to your purchase," says the small slip of paper. And indeed, the market tots it up along with the apples and Chee-tos, and transfers your electronic gift to a cumulative account. The transfer is anonymous—it doesn't have your name on it—and thus it assumes the aspect of digital cash. Our local Pathmark chain gathered 60,000 such electronic gifts for the Greater Philadelphia Food Bank during the Thanksgiving season. Not bad!

Online cash gifts are not quite so easy, since the mechanisms for digital cash are still evolving. Nevertheless, pioneering charities are already gearing up to accept such offerings:

- If you possess a CyberCash Wallet (*http://www.cybercash.com*), you can donate to Project Bosnia at Villanova University (*http://www.law.vill.edu/vcilp/bosnia*). During the 1996 primary season, cybernauts could support Charlie Sanders' (unsuccessful) bid to unseat North Carolina's archconservative senator, Jesse Helms.

- One of the most charming places to drop a little CyberCoin is *The Cyber Fridge,* a site where children create and display online art work in their very own gallery, and where purchases of art are donated to the Make a Wish Foundation (*http://penny.rwc.cybercash.com/kidpics*).

- Some "e-cash" can be spent at sites that have worked out an arrangement with the Digicash organization (*http://www.digicash.com*). One amusing pitch (now defunct, alas) came from the Virtual Beggar site which proclaimed "just when you thought you could escape the realities of the real world, here I am, the first beggar in cyberspace. I promise not to put your donations to good use. I'll probably use the money to feed one of the habits that helps keep me here on the streets." However, the message went on, if you want to "really help" a click will take you to a hotlinked list of organizations that really help the homeless. The Dorothy Day House and the St. Vincent de Paul Village were on the list, along with the National Coalition for the Homeless.

Auctions, Games, and Gambling

We haven't quite come across a church bingo parlor in cyberspace, but we have no doubt something like it will appear at any time. Consider the following:

- The Canadian Museum of Civilization (*http://www.cmcc.muse.digital.ca/cmc/cmceng/welcmeng.html*) held a "Sponsor a Treasure" online auction. Every week a new museum treasure was put up for "adoption," and the price of the adoption was open for bidding. Members could bid to sponsor an artifact, and their reward would be public recognition whenever it was displayed. The money bid was not collected online, but was treated as a pledge.

- Charitable organizations—and even libraries—are even more likely to cozy up to the idea of online auctions, since such devices are already an accepted fundraising practice. In late 1995, AmeriCares, an international relief organization, persuaded eighty merchants to put up merchandise for auction over the Internet. Viewers could see an item, see the latest bid, and enter their own bids. The winners were notified when the auction closed and asked to send in their payment. By now, such auctions could rely on a secure credit card mechanism, and in the future digital cash may come into play. For a look at online auctions for stamp, art, and antique collectors, see the list of commercial sites at the Internet Auction List (*http://www.usaweb.com/auction.html*).

- The Riddler site (*http://www.riddler.com*) contains games of chance and skill, scavenger hunts, trivia contests, and crossword puzzles. Players compete for actual prizes, ranging from books to cars. According to an article in *Internet World* (February 1997) the site has attracted more than 185,000 players and awarded more than $325,000 in prizes. Players do not have to pony up any wagers. Instead each player registers with the site by filling out a detailed form. "The idea is to collect lots of juicy demographic data about the players and to serve it up to advertisers eager to flash their banners at target markets."

- The Coeur d'Alene tribe—which already has a bingo hall and casino on its reservation in Idaho—made its gambling move to cyberspace with a site that offers blackjack and lotto (*www.uslottery. com*). The tribe has decided that 10 percent of its gambling profits will go to tribes who don't have gambling income, and 25 percent will be used to buy back land from non-Indians. The balance will be used for social services and educational programs (*New York Times* 7/5/97).

- Serious gambling is happening on several sites that are based in other countries, but available to players worldwide. The Interactive Gaming and Communications Corporation, based in Grenada, runs Global Casino at *http://www.gamblenet.com*. Tiny Liechtenstein has started a world lottery at *http://www.interlotto.li*; and the Antigua-based World Wide Web Casinos hosts Net Pirates at *http://www.netpirates.com*. Such enterprises are working to create a consensus that allows and validates Internet gambling. If that happens, watch for St. Bartholomew's to move its bingo parlor to cyberspace.

Think Big   So there you have it. Gambling, games, and CyberCash. The Internet awash in money—or at least that's the vision for the future. If this vision seems far-fetched, consider this fact: a stupendous amount of electronic money is already flowing online. This flow is between banks, as they use private wires to shift funds among themselves. Credit cards are also plugged into this system, as are the central banks of each nation.

To get some idea of the immensity of this flow, consider two figures: several nondescript buildings in Secaucus, New Jersey, are the central switching stations for interbank electronic transactions. This "Secaucus Corridor" handles almost 90 percent of the routine monthly deductions and payments that people establish through their checking accounts— or three billion transactions a year. The Secaucus Corridor moves more than $600 billion each and every day, and across the river in New York, $2 trillion is handled every day (*New York Times*, 2/18/97). The banks and the major credit card companies are quite used to handling money over the wire, and as soon as the Internet "wire" becomes a little more secure and a little more robust and a little more comfortable for consumers big sums will begin to flow.

As we have indicated, electronic commerce should lead to electronic charitable giving. The more people pull out their cyberwallets or click the "e-cash" payment option, the more they will consider sending money to your institution, school, or cause. You can *bet* on it :) and now is the time to start thinking about possibilities for your development operation.

PART II

Seeing
the Sites

4

The Red Cross:
A Comprehensive Site

The American Red Cross (*www.redcross.org*) has created a model non-profit Web site which should be studied by anyone who wants to use the Internet for fundraising and public relations. It is well designed, downloads quickly, and contains just about everything that one could imagine wanting. It is also well managed and kept up-to-the-minute with breaking news. The site as you visit it today will no doubt differ from our description here. However, the fundamentals of fundraising excellence on the Web will remain.

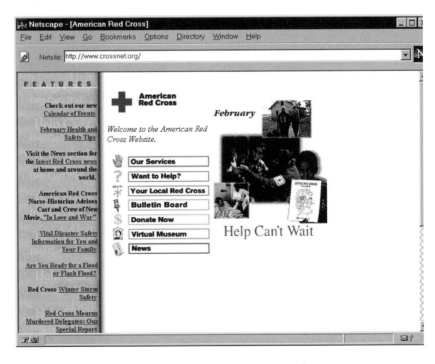

The Main Page

While the Red Cross does many things, it is best known for its work with natural and human-made disasters. Therefore a crucial element of its site is that it contain timely and accurate information about such situations. A key strategy for this site, as for any disaster or relief agency, is that visitors can quickly:

> find out what happened;
>
> find out what the Red Cross is doing about it;
>
> find out what "you can do" about it, including volunteering; and
>
> donate on the spot.

All of these options are clearly and elegantly built in to the home page. The left column lists breaking crises. Click and you will go to full descriptions of who, what, when, and what to do. The center list quickly takes the viewer to the main sections of the site, each of which is identified by color and by an icon. The sections are:

Our Services, which connects to a "What We Do" page that describes and links to the major activities of the Red Cross.

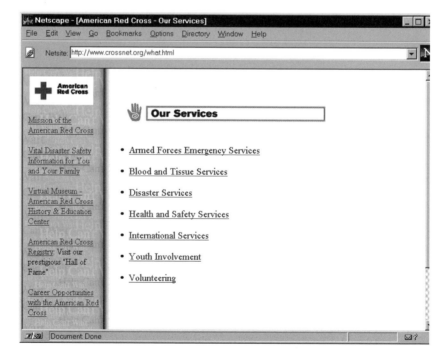

Want to Help? which brings up links to monetary donations, but also to blood donations, to tissue donation, and to "Helping others makes you feel good. Find out why, right now."

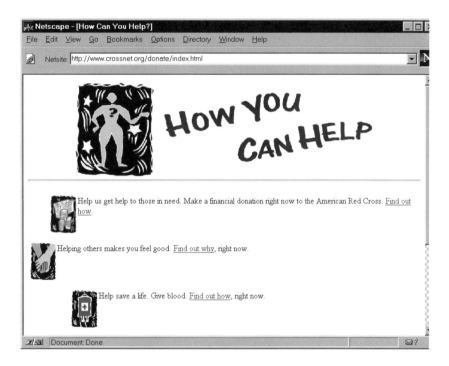

Your Local Red Cross, which allows you to search for your local chapter by entering your zip code.

Bulletin Board, a page that functions as a combination "What's New" and Red Cross Sampler, and gives over twenty links to interesting pages, including "Career Opportunities," "Repair Your Flooded Home," "A Day in the Life of the Red Cross," "Volunteer," and a multimedia (video) welcome from the Red Cross president.

Donate Now, which allows viewers to donate online using a major credit card, or instructs people on how to donate by phone and by mail.

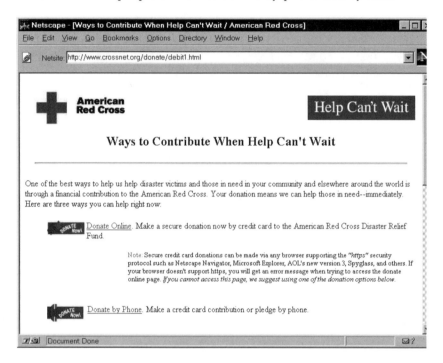

Virtual Museum, which allows readers to learn about the American Red Cross by time period, and which also contains an "automated slide show" that takes the viewer to important moments in Red Cross history.

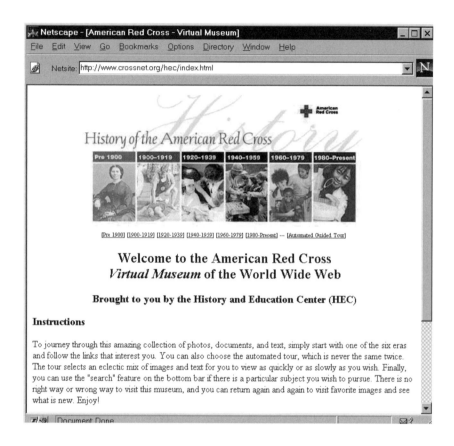

News, which features late-breaking stories, and links to other stories, as well as to a searchable news archive. In early 1997 this page contained top stories on the hostage crisis in Peru, the severe storms in the Northwest, and the killing of six Red Cross workers in Chechnya. From our experience in visiting this site many times, the top stories can literally change overnight and include links to Web-based CNN coverage of events.

Finally, the home page contains icon links to a "Feedback" page and a "Search" mechanism. At the bottom of every page in the Red Cross site is a bar containing ten icons that allow the visitor to jump quickly to major locations:

Special Features

Searching

The Red Cross site has a powerful and sophisticated search engine. This is the technical name for a software program that quickly runs through the files on the Red Cross server and finds what you need. A simple keyword search on *storm,* for example, yielded a string of well-organized pages covering recent storm emergencies, including Hurricane Opal, the Northwest floods, and "Winter Storm Safety Tips." Every result was hotlinked so that a simple click would take the viewer to the relevant text.

No matter how well organized, every large Web site needs a good search mechanism. Sophisticated visitors—and there are more of us each day—will often use your search engine rather than follow your table of contents or your clever icons. Frankly, it's faster than clicking through a lot of intermediate pages, and therefore more efficient. At present the Web has scores of search engines, and some of them are dreadful. Eventually, two or three search engines will come to dominate the pack, and searching will become an important element in all substantive sites. The Red Cross is a leader in this regard.

Making Gifts

The Red Cross is one of the first large agencies to allow online donations, using your American Express, Visa, or MasterCard. In early 1997 this was accomplished through a "secure" Netscape system, though additional mechanisms will no doubt come into play as the Visa/MasterCard SET security system becomes standardized. It makes a lot of sense for a disaster relief agency to allow on-the-spot immediate donations, since people want to make a gift when alarm or compassion is running high. While a torrent of gifts may not arrive via the Internet in the next few years, we predict that the pace of charitable gift-giving will match the pace of online commerce, and that in three to five years this will be *very* significant. (For a discussion of online gifts and the "security" red herring, see chapter 3.)

Involvement

The Red Cross has built in a number of interactive "involvement" devices. Besides allowing online gifts, which is a form of concrete action, the site also encourages volunteerism. Generally this is done by helping the visitor find his or her local chapter and suggesting a phone call or visit. The Los Angeles chapter lists its volunteer opportunities online, so that people can see if their skills match up. The Philadelphia chapter has a link especially for Internet-skilled volunteers, which allows interested parties to register their skills and interests online.

With over 1.4 million volunteers serving in 1995, the Red Cross provides a spectacular example of a volunteer-based service organization. As a general rule, the organization has elected not to allow people to "volunteer" online, since a face-to-face interview is no doubt preferable. Some agencies might want to allow volunteers to "apply" by filling out online forms, and follow up with an interview.

There are other involvement mechanisms as well. The "Feedback" icon leads to a page that allows direct submission of questions and comments to the national chapter, as well as comments about the Web site. These feedback mechanisms are common to most Web sites nowadays, and allow the visitor to communicate with your organization directly. Even the smallest and least sophisticated site can employ a few keystrokes to create a "mailto" link that will allow such communication, so be sure to build it into your site.

Knowing that so many lives have been touched by the Red Cross, the national chapter goes a step further and includes the following capability:

> *Share Your Red Cross Stories.* Every day, the American Red Cross helps someone in need—responding to emergencies down the street . . . across the country . . . around the world. Your Red Cross is a part of your community, but we wouldn't be there without you. To let you know how much we appreciate your support, we'd like to feature your story on our Web site. So e-mail your story today to editor@usa.redcross.org and let us know how the Red Cross made a difference in your life or in your community.

In conclusion, we cannot say enough about the excellence, design sophistication, and good sense behind this site. For the moment, if you can visit only one nonlibrary nonprofit site, make it the Red Cross!

5

Libraries on the Web: Friends, Public Relations, and Events

Libraries of all sizes and stripes are taking to the Internet to find friends, tell their story, and promote events. We will take the Penn Library's development pages (*http://www.library.upenn.edu/friends*) as an illustration. In creating the site, we began with a very different strategy than did the Red Cross. They created a serious site, aimed at a potential mass audience. We created an experimental, even playful, site which was initially intended for a handful of viewers. Their long-range fundraising strategy was aimed at gathering a large number of small gifts. Ours was aimed at stimulating a small number of large gifts. Their site had to represent the entire organization. Our site did not have to bear such a heavy responsibility and could be buried within the library's huge Web structure.

As an example, for almost two years, our site has contained a sponsorship link to a mythical record company—MacDuff International. We wanted to show our colleagues what such a corporate link would look like and to test their reaction, so we imagined that MacDuff (whose motto was "Play on, MacDuff") had supported our project to build a Music Center in memory of Marian Anderson. We also imagined that MacDuff had its own company foundation, and that the foundation had a home page that included links to the wonderful projects that it supported—all of which happened to be at Penn. This entire minisite (which is labeled as mythical) can be seen at *http://www.library.upenn.edu/friends/anderson. html* and on the CD that accompanies this book.

After our first year of operation, we began to reorganize our site. This major makeover is still in progress, so we recommend a current visit in order to have a full picture of what we are doing.

The Penn Library's "Friends and Benefactors" site differs from the Red Cross site in a variety of interesting ways. Here's some jargon: The Penn Library development site is a comprehensive, embedded, information-rich Web site with an Intranet bias.

Here's the translation:

Intranet bias: When we were building the site, we decided that our first audience would be the on-campus community—what some people are now terming the "Intranet" in contrast to the global "Internet." That meant that we could assume most of our viewers would be able to load and display our pages at high speed, and therefore that we could create pages with lots of graphics. The Red Cross is more focused on an "Internet" audience, most of whom may visit at very low speed. As our site has become more popular, we have begun to redesign our pages for modem access.

Embedded: A site can have its pages embedded or enmeshed in a larger institutional site, which means that it will have links from many locations in the larger site. In the case of our "Friends and Benefactors" site, it can be reached from the main Library page, from "What's New," from the Special Collections home page, from "Exhibitions and Programs," and in a variety of other ways. The advantage of an embedded site is that people will stumble on it while cruising the larger system.

Information-rich: An information-rich site has plenty of text and/or data and/or graphics that are of interest to your constituents. Libraries with online resources are quintessential examples. Such sites are visited again and again and can be thought of as "repeat sites." The Red Cross has a significant amount of useful and regularly updated information on its pages, but this pales in comparison with a good cyberlibrary.

Comprehensive: The "Friends and Benefactors" site attempts to be a full development site, covering our major fundraising goals and projects. It also has a pledge site, an online membership form, an events calendar, and a series of donor recognition pages. The Red Cross is also a comprehensive fundraising site, though donations for particular projects or initiatives are not emphasized—rather, their emphasis is on "general" (unrestricted) donations.

We will not undertake a complete review of the Penn Library site, but will focus instead on its use for constituency building, event promotion, and public relations.

The Friends Pages

An important goal of the library is to build its "Friends" organization—what others might call their "membership." In this regard, we have several tasks in mind for the Web site:

1. We want the site to keep our Friends informed of library news, as well as programs and events.
2. We want the site to "recognize" and celebrate the contributions that Friends make to the library.
3. We want the site to gather new Friends.

The library's Friends are a very important constituency, but not primarily because they pay annual dues or respond to our annual appeal. The amount of money that we raise or hope to raise from Friends' annual gifts is minor ($50,000 to $100,000) compared to our overall fundraising goals ($2 million to $5 million each year).

The Friends are important because many of our major gift donors will come from among the Friends. In addition, many Friends are reunion class leaders, and these classes have made millions of dollars in gifts to the library. Also a significant number of important collection (book and manuscript) gifts have come from card-carrying Friends. Finally, the Friends provide us with consistent feedback and link the library with the wider community.

So the more Friends the merrier, and the easier it is to become a Friend, the better. With this in mind, we have created a new membership category called the "E-Friend." E-Friends can join online and are not asked to pay a membership fee. A special button was created and sprinkled throughout our pages, saying "I want to be an E-Friend!"

Click on the button and you are taken to an online form for joining. Fill it out, click "send," and you are part of our wired membership.

Generally, we respond by e-mail immediately, so the membership is cheap, painless, and fast. From then on you receive alerts to library events, word of cool new library cyberservices, bulletins about library gifts, Web postcards—and who knows what else we will think up?

It is also possible to join the regular Friends online. In this case, the visitor clicks on a "Join the Friends" link and is presented with a form

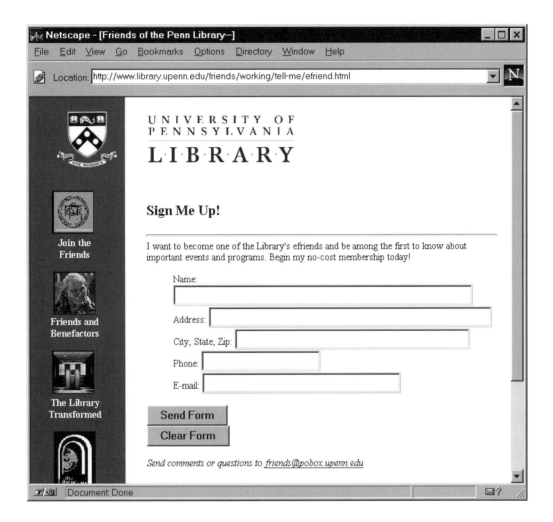

that allows her to indicate what level of membership she would like to have. We do not currently request or allow online credit card payments, but instead simply bill new members for their dues.

We have seen many sites that invite the prospective member to print out the form, fill it out by hand, and mail it in with a check. This seems foolish to us. A person who is at your site and wants to join should be able to do so then and there, even if you have to bill him or her. For most of us the membership fee is secondary, anyway. The highest priority is in gathering the new Friend, who can then become an active source of support for many years to come.

We plan to experiment with the E-Friend concept over the next several years. Our university has a very widespread alumni base—literally, it is worldwide. Our traditional Friends organization has relied upon geographical proximity to the campus. However, our E-Friends program can reach out to every corner of the planet.

The new possibilities presented by electronic membership may be even more promising for organizations such as the Sierra Club, the National Organization of Women, or the Christian Coalition. For the library, we can imagine many future directions for our E-Friend effort, including:

- book reviews and Web site reviews, prepared by library staff or Friends and communicated to the entire list;
- a "Question & Answer" Web site, where Friends' queries can be answered by library staff;
- a "Bulletin Board" site, where E-Friends can post comments, questions, and ideas, and where other E-Friends can reply. This would be similar to an Internet "news" site;
- an E-Friends "listserv," where postings are automatically sent to all E-Friends (this is both more intrusive and more engaging than a bulletin board);
- a "Friends Forum," where E-Friends can periodically engage in live Internet exchanges with library leaders, authors, and professors; and
- a "Friends Chat Room," where any E-Friend can engage with any other E-Friend in real time, while others watch or jump in and add their two cents' worth. Such "chat" capacities have been popular with Internet service providers like America Online.

We have also placed the Friends Calendar online. Many of the events have live links to a more detailed description of the undertaking. In the case of the calendar entry for the Illustrated Books exhibit, for example, viewers could also clink on a link to the online "virtual" version of the exhibit.

We also have created "RSVP" buttons at each upcoming event. This allows Friends to let us know if they plan to attend a particular event. (Most Friends events are free to members; the reason we ask for responses is in order to get an estimated count for refreshments and room arrangements.)

A Friends and/or members site can be a very full and interactive site, limited only by your time and your imagination. Ideas we are considering include a list of the Friends leaders, perhaps with their pictures and e-mail addresses, and a "Message from the Friends' President" page, where updated news can be placed. We are currently putting the Friends newsletter online, along with an archive of past issues (*http://www.library. upenn.edu/friends/members/*).

Most organizations that take the trouble of establishing a Web site will want to consider some form of online membership. Why not? Such new friends are wonderful prospects for fundraising!

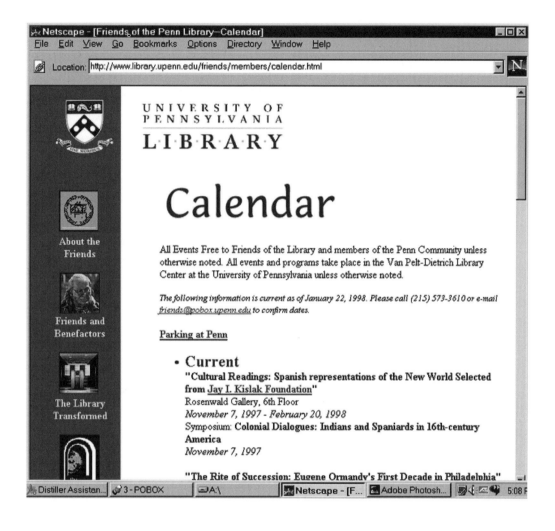

Netscape - [Friends of the Penn Library—Calendar]

File   Edit   View   Go   Bookmarks   Options   Directory   Window   Help

Location: http://www.library.upenn.edu/friends/members/calendar.html

UNIVERSITY OF PENNSYLVANIA
L·I·B·R·A·R·Y

About the
Friends

Friends and
Benefactors

The Library
Transformed

Calendar

All Events Free to Friends of the Library and members of the Penn Community unless
otherwise noted. All events and programs take place in the Van Pelt-Dietrich Library
Center at the University of Pennsylvania unless otherwise noted.

*The following information is current as of January 22, 1998. Please call (215) 573-3610 or e-mail
friends@pobox.upenn.edu to confirm dates.*

Parking at Penn

- ## Current
  **"Cultural Readings: Spanish representations of the New World Selected
  from Jay I. Kislak Foundation"**
  Rosenwald Gallery, 6th Floor
  November 7, 1997 - February 20, 1998
  Symposium: **Colonial Dialogues: Indians and Spaniards in 16th-century
  America**
  November 7, 1997

  "The Rite of Succession: Eugene Ormandy's First Decade in Philadelphia"

Distiller Assistan... | 3 - POBOX | A:\ | Netscape - [F... | Adobe Photosh... | 5:08 P

The Metropolitan Museum of Art (*http://www.metmuseum.org*) obviously feels that gathering new friends, and even new acquaintances, is of value.

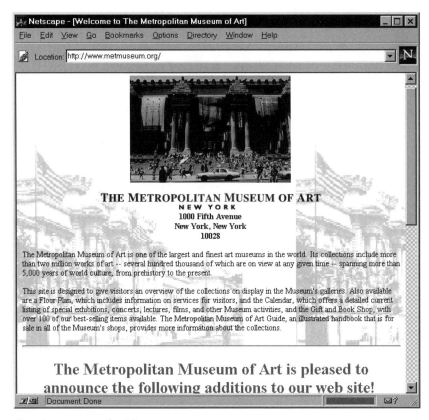

Opening page at the Met

The primary emphasis of the Met's Web strategy appears to be to use its site to gather members, or at least to capture the e-mail addresses of visitors. The first clickable option, in large print, is to become a "Met Net Member."

Click on "Membership" and the visitor is given a choice of Become a Member, Events for Members, Corporate Entertaining, and Travel. Click on "Become a Member" and the following "special announcement" appears:

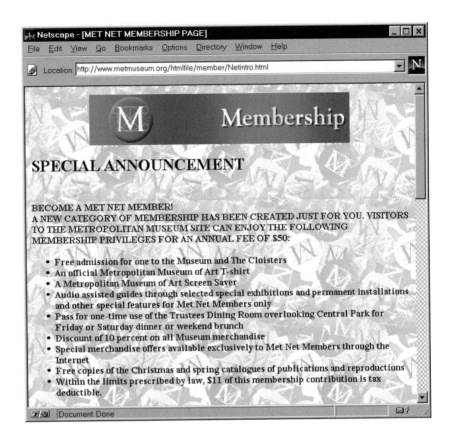

Not bad for 50 bucks! Other membership categories are listed, from "Student" ($35) all the way up to "Patron Circle" at $7,000. Next to each level of membership is an "order here" button, which takes the visitor through the Museum shop to "purchase" a membership using a credit card.

The second option on the Met's home page is to visit the Museum gift shop. The third clickable option is to get "instructions" on how to access Net Member benefits. Only after a new section on education does the visitor have the chance to see the collections or check the exhibit calendar. Before seeing the collections, the new visitor is invited to "register" before entering the museum. This registration is nice and simple, consisting of a brief form that allows you to leave your name and e-mail address. No doubt the Met has promotional plans for this list, which is likely to grow very quickly.

Events and Public Relations

During Penn's 1996 Homecoming the library hosted a "Showcase" in partnership with the Alumni Affairs Office. This event was designed to introduce alumni and parents to the new and exciting services of the library system, especially the electronic services. The Showcase included an "Open House" at sixteen libraries, eight hours of "Live Internet Theater" presentations in our Class of '55 projection conference room, a star-studded symposium entitled "What's Playing on the Celestial Jukebox," and an online student "Great Web Hunt."

We made extensive use of the Web to publicize and promote the event. We created a "Library Showcase" site (contained on the companion CD), which had the calendar of events, with times and locations. The symposium speakers were profiled, accompanied by their pictures, and with links to their personal home pages. The Great Web Hunt had its own linked home page, with rules of the contest, and a schedule for the various rounds of play. The search questions were released to the Web site at a specified time, and a special form was established for visitors who wanted to "play" online.

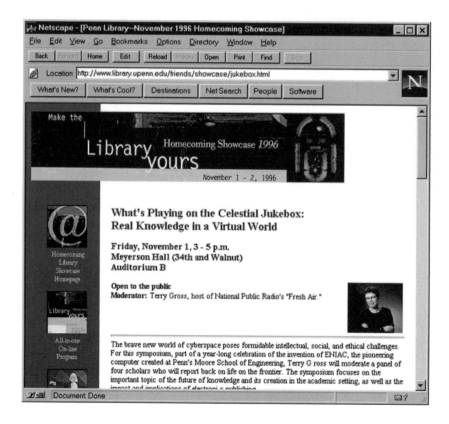

The moderator for the symposium, Terry Gross of NPR's *Fresh Air* program, recorded the show for later broadcast. We also distributed video- and audiotapes of the panel to our Friends of the Library. Finally, a printed transcript of the symposium—which focused on the use of the Internet for scholarly communication—was printed as an issue of the *Penn Library News,* and a Web version was mounted at *http://www.library. upenn.edulibpubs/Penn_Lib_News_Symp/symp1.html.*

In this example, then, a Web site was used to promote and enhance a real-life event. But a Web site can also be an "event" in itself. This was the case with our Marian Anderson site, which was unveiled around the time of her 100th birthday (February 27, 1997).

To celebrate this occasion, the Penn Library mounted an extensive Web exhibition based upon material from our Anderson Archives. Visitors can learn the story of her life and see scores of photographs from every stage of her career. Further, they can hear eight audio excerpts from an unpublished interview with the great singer and hear three of her songs. They can also see video newsreel footage of her singing "My Country 'tis of Thee" at the Lincoln Memorial in 1939. (The Web address is *http:// www.library.upenn.edu/special/gallery/anderson/*)

Newspapers, television, radio, and library journals around the country picked up the press release on this site. The Philadelphia *Inquirer* did an extensive article based on the Anderson Web site, and that story was used in many Knight-Ridder newspapers throughout the United States. Enthusiastic e-mail comments came from all over the country, and from outside the country, and still are coming in today.

The online exhibit is a very powerful new public relations and educational tool for libraries, museums, and other cultural organizations. The Penn Library's Department of Special Collections is one of the pioneers in this area, and as of this writing has mounted more than ten full exhibition sites (see *http://www.library.upenn.edu/special/events.html*).

When the fiftieth anniversary of the development of the ENIAC computer at Penn's Moore School of Electrical Engineering was being celebrated, an exhibition on coinventor John W. Mauchly was mounted in the Rosenwald Gallery. A parallel online exhibition (*http://www.library.upenn. edu/special/gallery/mauchly/jwmintro.html*) was also created. This online exhibition went further than the physical display. It included dozens of links to the online *Encyclopaedia Britannica,* which provided definitions and greater detail on important scientific terms. Click on the term "vacuum tube" and up would pop a hotlinked list of related articles, such as "Computers: History of Computing: Modern Electronic Digital Computers: Early Vacuum Tube Devices." The exhibition also had links to related Internet resources, such as the recollections of coinventor J. Presper Eckert at the Smithsonian Institution's Web site.

The Mauchly exhibition has drawn attention from many corners of the globe. The exhibition contains a "comments" line that allows viewers to e-mail a response. The library has heard from viewers in Sweden, Italy, and Australia, to name but a few. In one case a researcher said that the online material added to his research on the development of early computers. In another instance a teacher asked for permission to download and use in his teaching several of the historical photographs that were part of the presentation (we said that was fine).

Penn is not the only library to mount online exhibitions. Other instances of such exhibits can be found at the Library of Congress, and at Duke, the University of Michigan, and the University of Virginia. (See *http://sunsite.berkeley.edu/Collections/*)

From a scholarly point of view, online exhibitions can be the "front door" to far more extensive material. There is every reason to think that libraries and other cultural institutions can use such exhibitions to draw the viewer further into the subject. For example, most exhibitions are limited in terms of the number of images and the amount of text that can be displayed in the physical space that is available in a gallery or hall. Not so in cyberspace. Any number of images and any amount of written commentary can be provided, along with audio and video clips. In addition, links can be provided to related online material, or to other holdings that can be viewed on-site.

In addition to their scholarly function, and their interest to the general public, online exhibitions are also a wonderful way to link a donor with his or her gift. As an example of such "donor recognition" see the extensive "Household Words" exhibit of Esther Bradford Aresty's cookbook and culinary arts collection (see *http://www.library.upenn.edu/special/gallery/aresty/aresty1.html*).

Prior to the advent of the World Wide Web, the donor of an important collection might have the pleasure of knowing that a special label recognizing her gift would be placed with each volume, that the collection would be named in her honor, and that this name would appear on the catalog entry. In some cases, the donor could receive recognition through an exhibition and related catalog. And in rare instances, the collection might be the subject for an illustrated book—though such publications are quite expensive and usually have very limited print runs.

Now that the Web allows libraries to mount collections online, the donor can have her name associated with the active use of her materials by students and scholars worldwide. This new and vital prominence for the collection—and the person or family who painstakingly assembled it—adds an exciting dimension to stewardship for the gift. Most importantly, it continues to associate the donor with the public use of the collection, and for most donors there can be no greater satisfaction.

Are Public Libraries Different?

As part of the research for our book, we looked at how public libraries are using the Web for friend-raising and fundraising. We found that, although public libraries are online in increasing numbers, their use of their Web sites for fundraising or friend-raising is very much in the formative stages. To survey the state of this issue in public libraries nationwide, we took an nth-name sample of 100 libraries from the Milton (Massachusetts) Public Library's list of libraries online (*http://web0.tiac.net/users/mpl/public. libraries.html*). We found that the majority of sites mention a Friends organization, volunteer opportunities, advocacy activities, or giving opportunities, but that the quantity of information offered is in most part fairly limited. In interviews with public library staff, we found a very modest level of enthusiasm for investing resources in Web-based fundraising.

Given that many public libraries have experienced cutbacks in staff, slowdowns in funding, and legislative blind eyes in keeping up with physical plant maintenance, this may not be surprising. After all, if a local librarian faces a choice between staying open on Saturday or building an experimental Web site, what's to debate?

We also found some level of skepticism about the financial results of such an investment. Consider this comment by the public relations manager of a large public library: "We have had a presence on the Library's Web page for a year now and have received thirteen donations. From my own experience and in talking with colleagues and reading topical literature, I have found that it is good to have a presence for informational/educational purposes, but that the Web is not the place to look to for contributions at present. Given the nature of philanthropy, it appears that donors are not yet comfortable with this medium as a vehicle for giving. I'd say we're probably a minimum of three to five years away from seeing any significant income from a Web site."

We agree with this time frame. Keeping in mind that the statement was made in early 1997, that would suggest an altered landscape by 2000 or 2002. We also agree that the number of direct online gifts will be modest. But, as we hope we have made clear by now, that is only one use of the Web for fundraising and friend-raising.

The cost threshhold for getting on the Web is becoming ever more modest. The rise of Web-authoring skills among our constituents is spectacular. A public library can start a Web site with a $25-a-month Internet service provider and a bright high school volunteer. Many of the ideas and stratagems that we suggest in this book are directly applicable to even the smallest public library.

We found several sites that indicate the directions that public libraries are taking:

Alachua County (Florida) Library District
http://www.acld.lib.fl.us/

This public library system has a Friends organization with a history dating back more than forty years, as well as a separate foundation for fundraising purposes. The system's home page includes an entire friend-raising section linking financial contributions with gifts of time. Titled "Ways to Help Your Library," it includes sections on how to make a gift to your library; learning about the Library Foundation; joining the Friends of the Library; and volunteering your time. A series of well laid-out text-only pages engagingly presents the history, aims, accomplishments, and aspirations of both Friends and Foundation, recognizing past and present volunteers and offering suggestions for becoming involved. The section on the semiannual book sale is of particular interest.

Friends of the Oakland (California) Public Library
http://www.hugin.imat.com/~fopl/

This separate Friends organization offers both advocacy and financial support. Its well-conceived Web site provides information on both programs, including its fundraising programs, the purposes of its gifts, and its work in expanding access to the library collections and in shaping the year's budget. It offers information on joining the Friends at a variety of giving levels, as well as an address to which to send dues. An informative page on its bookstore gives directions and a list of nearby eateries. Another page lists bookstores offering discounts to Friends members. Although there is no form for joining online, the necessary information is there; moreover, the surfer can e-mail the president of the Friends group directly from the Web site.

This site also can serve as an inspiration for libraries who are concerned about their level of Web-weaving expertise: its use of graphics is limited to its initial home-page logo and some colorful horizontal separators, yet the overall effect is welcoming and pleasing to the eye.

Rochester Hills (Michigan) Public Library
http://metronet.lib.mi.us/ROCH/rhpl.html

Access to the Friends of the Library information is through the "Library Information" link on the home page. The Friends pages are attractive and informative, and references to the Friends are scattered among other pages on the site. This site includes photographs of Friends and their activities. The Friends section includes information on the bookstore, the Friends-sponsored "Authors in April" program of school visits, and the graduate scholarship in library science.

Los Angeles Public Library
http://www.lapl.org

> The Los Angeles Public Library (LAPL) has both a separate Friends orga-
> nization and a separate Foundation for fundraising purposes. The first
> link from LAPL's home page, "General Information about the Los Angeles
> Public Library," offers links to five "friend-raising" pages or sections: li-
> brary programs and exhibits; the library store; the joint annual report of
> the LAPL and its Foundation; the Library Foundation of Los Angeles;
> and Friends of the Los Angeles Public Library. The pages, in each case,
> offer basic information on whom to contact to join the Friends, buy from
> the bookstore, reach the Foundation. The Annual Report recognizes in-
> dividual, corporate and foundation donors in an omnibus listing.

New York Public Library
http://www.nypl.org

> Not surprisingly, the country's largest public library has an attractive and
> well-designed Web site. The "membership" section is linked from its

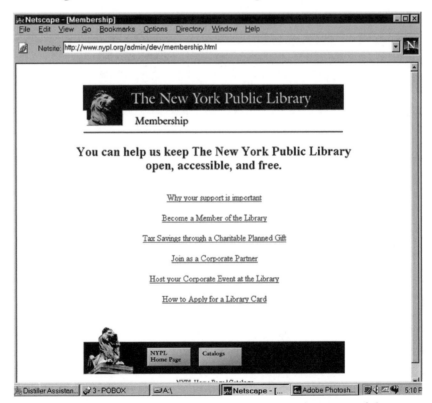

*New York Public Library's membership welcome page (Courtesy of the New
York Public Library)*

home page. The membership welcome page ties advocacy to giving in its opening line: "You can help us keep the New York Public Library open, accessible, and free."

Subsequent pages offer information on membership at varying levels and the benefits members can receive, with links leading to a print-and-mail-in order form. There's something to appeal to every category of potential donor, ranging from Friends through corporate partners and those interested in planned giving, along with e-mail links to the library's development office. In the fall of 1997, the NYPL launched a $500-million capital campaign. Stay tuned to its site for fundraising ideas.

In closing, here are some additional ideas for public libraries:

Recognize your "other donors."

The public library's friends may contribute one of three things, each important in its own way: money, time, and influence. Your friends include major donors when you have them, of course, but they also include the many volunteers who supplement the efforts of the library staff by shelving books or enrich the community by organizing library-based cultural events. They put together a book sale, run a bookstore, use their personal or political influence to safeguard or strengthen a library's budget.

Put up pages celebrating past Friends events such as book signings and link them from other parts of your site (making sure you flag them as "archives" so your site doesn't look stale). Create an online feature article about the bookstore—your production cost is measured in pennies compared to the cost of printing a newsletter, so you can afford it. Put up a page highlighting the benefits of a successful budget campaign, in the process thanking and even quoting the local officials who got behind the library budget and shoved, with recognition for those others who supported their efforts. Online recognition of these activities and the stakeholders who make them possible is another tool in recognizing these important nonmonetary gifts.

Everything that has been written in chapter 2 regarding major donors can be adapted to these other kinds of "donors" in a public library setting. If a volunteer has single-handedly brought about a worthwhile new program, showcase it and her with a Web page or section. Print it out and put it in a handsome presentation binder; download it to a floppy disk and present that as well as the binder; feature a link to the recognition site, possibly with a thumbnail head shot as the connecting link, on the library home page for a week. In fact, this leads us to a second important point, which is:

Showcase past events as well as announcing upcoming events.

There's nothing like a page including colorful pictures of an event to communicate the message that library events are worth attending. The commemoration of the event serves to recognize the efforts of the volunteers who put it together, or who made a program possible. Thanks to supermarket photoprocessors that will give you your photos on a floppy disk for a small fee, it's possible to add photos to a Web site without buying expensive equipment or software (see chapter 7 for more details).

Use the site, if possible, as an advocacy vehicle.

If the site is library based, there may be restrictions on the degree to which you can comment on policies affecting the library. In the case of an independent site such as the Friends of the Oakland Library mentioned above, though, the separation makes it possible for the site to make the case for increased funding, new acquisitions, more space, longer hours, or special services. This is particularly important in a time when more and more reporters and other media professionals are turning to the World Wide Web to do their background research on a story. The Friends Web site, to the extent that policy permits, can be an articulate and constantly accessible spokesperson for its positions on key library issues.

Build your roster of Friends.

Begin by examining your "joining the Friends" section. If you have some lines of text giving an address or phone number of a contact person, consider creating a "print-and-mail-in-with-your-payment" document. Or, better yet, if you can use forms on your Web site create a "sign-me-up-and-bill-me" form. If you have the capability of creating an electronic mailing list, collect e-mail addresses so that you'll have a list of "E-Friends" to whom you can send library news and notices of upcoming events.

None of these Web-weaving suggestions is especially difficult to put into practice. They can all be done on a relatively low budget. There are commercial Internet service providers out there who can provide all the support needed for the activities listed above for monthly fees as low as $24.95 (including Web server space).

Everything a public library does now to strengthen its friend-raising activities and the visibility of its Friends on the World Wide Web will position it to make a shift from friend-raising to fundraising when its audience is ready to do business on the Web.

6

Rich Sites and Cool Sites

Think of it: the Web holds over hundreds of millions, maybe by now even billions, of pages for your perusal. Most of these pages are available free, and by the time you have plumbed their riches, hundreds of millions (or maybe billions) of new pages will have been added.

Of course, a lot of these pages are junk, and an even greater number are on topics that will interest only a tiny handful of people, yet the variety at the average reader's disposal is simply staggering.

Readers of this book will be wondering how their site can compete with all the wondrous sites on the Net. We believe the answer is: your site must be "rich."

Fortunately, there are a variety of "riches" on the Web. Rich sites contain material that attracts viewers and builds repeat traffic. We classify them in four broad areas:

- Information-rich
- Involvement-rich
- Product-rich
- Entertainment-rich

Most nonprofit organizations will do well if they focus their energies on building sites that are *information-rich* and *involvement-rich*. Conversely, most of us will fare poorly if we try to compete with heavily financed product-rich and entertainment-rich sites.

Information-Rich Sites

A library with a wide range of digital online material is an obvious example of an information-rich site. Viewers come to such sites to gather information on a broad range of topics and for a wide variety of purposes. Just as in the physical realm, a good library site will be visited again and again by its customers.

A very different sort of information-rich site has been mounted by Amnesty International (*www.amnesty.org*). On their site one can find out about current high-focus campaigns, read the latest bulletins on human rights triumphs and tragedies, and search through an extensive archive of detailed country-by-country reports. Their "Act Now" section features three current prisoner-of-conscience campaigns and tells you where to send letters for their release. For people who are concerned about human rights, this information is of great value, and AI does not have to put a lot of "bells and whistles" on its site to attract viewers.

Most nonprofit organizations should place their first emphasis on information that will be of interest to their current and potential constituents. If you are a relief organization, your site should be up-to-date on the latest crises you are facing. If you are a cultural organization, you should have information on your current exhibition, show, performance, or special event. If you are a shelter for battered women, you should provide vital information on how to contact your staff at all hours, on what to do in an emergency, on how to find counseling.

The information that you provide does not have to be of interest to the entire world; it just has to be valuable for your particular constituency. Or perhaps we should say, constituencies. There are the people you serve and the people you hope will support you. There are the people you hope to educate, and perhaps the media. There are the people in your town, your region, your country, as well as your field, your profession, or your cause.

Most of us who work in fundraising or public relations are already busy generating and distributing information to our various constituencies. Think about how that information can be placed on a Web site, and take it from there.

Examples of information-rich sites can be found in Appendix A of this book and on the companion CD.

Involvement-Rich Sites

The Web is not just capable of delivering information, it is at its most powerful when it allows for *interaction*. Such interactions can be very simple—filling out a form, posting a question, making a suggestion—or they can be highly complex and even magical.

Any NPO that is considering the creation or expansion of a Web site should think creatively about utilizing the interactive capabilities of the

Internet. In particular, you should think about mechanisms that further the involvement of your constituents, since involvement often leads to identification with your organization, and identification leads to loyalty.

For example, Princeton University (*www.princeton.edu*) has created an alumni site that allows graduates to sign on to a "bulletin board" where they can correspond via e-mail with other members of their class. These sites allow for a kind of rolling reunion, where members share stories and opinions, and ask whatever happened to good old Bill. Every college and university knows that bringing alums back to campus for reunions builds loyalty and leads to increased financial support—even though most of these "sons and daughters" spend most of their time talking to each other and ignoring the carefully planned "updates" and "briefings" that we provide. So why not create "reunions" in cyberspace?

The Sierra Club (*www.sierraclub.org*) takes another approach. Not only can concerned environmental activists learn about global warming, legislation, and the voting records of their representatives, but they can link directly to the e-mail address of their senator or representative and make their views known on the spot. The club also has tips on how to "bird-dog" public figures who aren't environmentally correct, and even suggests some chants for crowd scenes, including "Clean water, clean air, [bad guy's name] doesn't care!"

Therefore, when building your site, first get the information up and available, but also make sure to build in involvement mechanisms. And be prepared to cope with the problems of success. For instance, are you ready to respond to twenty-five e-mail comments or queries a day? How about fifty? How about a thousand?

Examples of involvement-rich sites can be found in Appendix A of this book and on the companion CD.

Product and Entertainment Sites

There is no way that a nonprofit organization can or should attempt to compete with a product site. Such sites can invest in expensive window-dressing, complex ordering software, secure firewalled commerce servers, and twenty-four-hour online customer service.

On the other hand, if you do offer products and premiums as part of your income-generating mix in the physical world, you can certainly consider doing so in cyberspace.

The Metropolitan Museum has its "Shop" on line at *www.metmuseum.org*.

Clickable "hooks" to the Shop are located on many of its pages. When we dropped in, the large chinese export mugs and the footed bowl were prominently displayed. The online catalog offered selections of "Jewelry," "Posters and Prints," as well as items grouped "For the Holidays" and "For the Kids." Next to every item was an "Order Item" button that led to an online order form.

Many cultural institutions with large walk-in audiences have made good money from their shops. One thinks of the enticing shops in the Smithsonian museums, for example. Further, some institutions have managed to create a strong catalog business—the Met, the Boston Museum of Fine Arts, and National Public Radio are examples. Twenty years ago, it seemed wildly radical for a museum to organize a mail-order merchandise business. But now some institutions are making millions—in the case of the Metropolitan Museum, $80 million in gross receipts from shops and catalog sales in 1996, of which 10 to 12 percent is profit.

Keep in mind that selling online is not easy. It is a business, like any other, and will require an ongoing investment of time and money. The more the business grows, the more time and money it will take. Our advice is that you keep this aspect very simple, or contract it out to an experienced online vendor. (For example, FedEx will set up and maintain catalogs—and handle warehousing and shipping. See *www.fedex.com*)

Examples of nonprofit sites that offer products and/or premiums can be found in Appendix A of this book and on the companion CD.

As for entertainment sites, libraries and other nonprofit organizations should leave the razzle and dazzle to commercial vendors. One of our favorite quotes from the megamedia side of the Internet goes like this: "When it comes to the Web, entertainment is the 800-pound gorilla. Information is just a tiny little chihuahua."

The current gorilla in this category is none other than the Walt Disney site (*www.disney.com*). At this site you can download Disney cartoons, listen to Disney songs, book a vacation at Disney resorts, order books, get tickets to *Beauty and the Beast,* enter a "Family Fantasy" sweepstakes (win a vacation each year for five years), and on and on and on.

Most entertainment sites are designed as though the viewer has high-speed access to the site, yet most visitors are coming in through slow-speed phone lines. Thus a single two-minute preview for Disney's *Hunchback of Notre Dame* would have taken Adam over three hours to download and play on his 14.4 modem.

Of course, companies like Disney can afford to throw a few million dollars at their sites in order to establish themselves in cyberspace. They probably figure that they will learn valuable lessons to apply when high-bandwidth networks are finally in place, and the pot of gold is reached at the end of the rainbow.

Nonprofit organizations may occasionally want to use an entertainment gimmick to attract attention, as we did with an Internet scavenger hunt that we called "The Penn Library Great Web Hunt." We opened it to all students and offered a Pentium computer as the grand prize. The site received over a thousand hits in the few months that we had it mounted, and the library received some good publicity.

But caution is the byword. Let the 800-pound gorillas spend their millions and take their chances. Many companies have thrown money in every direction, have taken a low-brow, mass-audience approach to the Internet—and have gotten trampled in the process.

Perhaps an agile, thoughtful, small-is-beautiful, "chihuahua" approach isn't so bad.

Interactivity

Currently, media attention to the Web seems to be focused on bells and whistles. Attention is given to jazzy new applications such as Internet telephone conversations, stars that twinkle, billboards that scroll the news, audio and video "streaming," and sites that have a memory and can tell you what size shorts you wear.

We believe that the hallmarks of valuable Web sites will be less razzle-dazzle and more tangible: information, involvement, and interactivity.

Information sites are by definition "interactive" sites. Ask a question, get an answer; initiate a search, get the results. That is why library and other data-rich sites are already among the most heavily visited "storefronts" in cyberspace.

The truly significant advances in Web-weaving will come as developers discover what can be accomplished in the interactive mode. We believe that as interactivity takes hold, your Web site will move to the center of your communication process. Recently, Robert Pallone, Penn's Director of Development Information Services, circulated a list of ideas to consider for use in alumni relations activities. We think this list will give readers a few things to think about:

- Allow your constituents to update their personal information. Pallone's "Pennlink" alumni site (*http://alumni.dev.upenn.edu/alumni/start.html*) has found that younger alumni in particular like to keep their addresses, business affiliations, and phone numbers up-to-date in this manner.

- Create and maintain e-mail discussion lists. These lists could allow your alumni or constituents to:

    enjoy a general "talk" list;

    participate in thematic lists (sports, medicine, archeological digs, etc.);

    access a "Club" or "Chapter" list; or

    get work done through a board or volunteer/leader restricted list.

- Provide an electronic alumni directory, where your constituents could not only list their addresses and phone numbers, but could also have "clickable" e-mail and Web page addresses for instant communication.

- Enable "electronic data retrieval," for clubs and chapters, so that officers could download current mailing and contact lists.

- Create "electronic chat rooms" where constituents can interact "live" on any topic.

- Establish a "Q & A" site, where constituents can pose questions and the answers are posted for all to see. This can also be taken "live" and an online discussion with your president or director mounted at a particular date and time.

- Set up a "mentoring" and job placement site, where constituents can turn for assistance.

- Allow online ordering of organizational products, such as T-shirts, mugs, posters, and so on.

- Encourage online registration for events, dinners, tours, and so on.

- Publish class or club newsletters, with contributions from your constituents submitted by e-mail.

- Mount online surveys and other "opinion response vehicles."

- Host online courses and seminars. In 1996 the General Alumni Society offered a modern poetry course and a forum with the provost on "The Future of the University in the Information Age." Both were wildly successful.

To the above list, we would, of course, like to add:

- Allow online donations to the institution or its programs, using a pledge form, credit card, or "digital cash" (see chapter 3).

PART III

Your Web Publishing Program

7

Getting Started on Your Site

So, you may be saying to yourself at this point, I can see where a Web site can be useful in my development work. We can create an electronic storefront with information on our library; we can provide recognition to major donors and other important stakeholders; we can showcase our plans for the future; we can gather names of potential donors; we can even solicit gifts and pledges online. But how do I bring this about?

Fortunately, it's not hard. You can be up and running with a starter site within a week or so of the initial gleam in your eye, and you may not have to spend a cent (not counting your own time) to get started. Or you could call in a professional design firm and pay them a lot of money. Some smaller libraries have found Web-savvy folks in their Friends groups—folks who will be happy to get you up and running as part of their mission as Friends. If you have Web access, a computer with a word-processing package, and an online browser, you have everything you need to get started. Accounts with many Internet service providers entitle users to space on their Web servers; you may want to build your skills by developing a personal home page.

This chapter provides access to a collection of resources that will get you online with a maximum of impact and a minimum of misery.

Priorities for Building Your Site

Your first priorities in building a site are straightforward: Develop an online presence and a mechanism for feedback.

There are libraries out there that have been going to go online "in about six weeks" for the past two years. They are carefully weighing their priorities and conceptualizing their graphics approach and heaven only knows what else, but their sites are still going up "in about six weeks." Meanwhile, their potential donors, volunteers, and other stakeholders are passing them by—finding other organizations and other causes.

We would argue that it is better to go online with a modest site in short order than to wait to create the Mother of All Sites. The reasons? First, your audience can't find you if you're not there. Although presentation is important, content is crucial—and much of your audience will forgive a modest presentation if the content is there. Second, the experience you gain putting up your pages will shape the second iteration of your site, and this will happen much more quickly if you go ahead and develop that modest site than if you take weeks and months in initial planning. Remember, the goal here is "ready, fire, aim." Once you have a modest site up and running, too, you'll have built up some momentum that will make it easier to expand it.

Depending on the political climate at your library, you may need to involve a few people or many others in the approval process for your site. Site building is a kind of electronic publication, and one or more other people may need to be involved—but, unlike traditional publishing, you can always "stop the presses" and make a change. This is one of the real beauties of Web-building, and organizations that grasp this fact become somewhat more relaxed and flexible in their approach to their Web projects.

You can base your content planning on a very simple initial outline. Here's one as an example:

- Introduction to your library
    mission
    programs and services
    accomplishments

- Electronic case statement
    plans for the future
    current and future needs

- Hot topic (what's new)

- Donor recognition

- Becoming involved
    attending an event
    joining a Friends group
    signing up for a newsletter
    volunteering time
    making a donation

This or a similar outline can become the basis for your home page—an attractive, short-copy page offering links to these major sections. You could implement this outline on a simple site that involves a home page and several secondary pages. As you build additional pages, the secondary pages can be expanded to full sections with their own directories or folders in your file structure. Or, you could start really modestly with a home page and two secondary pages—one that introduces the organization and one that lists activities and provides information on becoming involved. You can add the other sections later.

What You Need:
Hardware, Software, Server Space

You can buy a lot of fancy equipment and software and a five-foot shelf of books to get started in Web publishing. Or you can bootstrap your way to your first Web site using manuals downloaded from the Web and your own mother wit. Here is the absolute minimum you need in the way of equipment and know-how:

- A computer with enough horsepower to run a graphical browser
- A graphical browser such as Netscape Navigator, Microsoft Internet Explorer, or even the built-in AOL browser
- Minimal knowledge of hypertext markup language (HTML), or an HTML editing program
- A word-processing program that lets you save as a text file
- Access to the Internet, including a file transfer program and space on a server
- A means of acquiring scanned images

Computer

For Web authoring—and by this we mean a combination of writing, design, and HTML coding—a fairly basic setup works perfectly well. Laura uses a high-powered machine at Penn, for example, but does a lot of her authoring at home on a Tandy 486 with 8 MB of memory and no special software. If you have a graphical browser on your computer, you have a powerful enough computer to do basic Web authoring.

Graphical Browser

At this point, the three browsers to consider are Netscape Navigator, Microsoft Internet Explorer, and the built-in AOL browser, which is simply a stripped-down version of an early version of Microsoft's product. At this writing, the World Wide Web Consortium is about to approve a new HTML standard, version 4.0, and features covered in this standard should be supported and displayed in the same ways by newer versions of Netscape and Explorer.

Knowledge of HTML

HTML is the set of codes which, when embedded in a text document, tell the browser how to display a file and how to retrieve linked files. It's not difficult to pick up, especially for older computer users who remember code-based word processing programs such as WordPerfect (remember "Reveal Codes?"). For folks who are uncomfortable without a graphical interface, there are add-on authoring programs for Microsoft Word and Netscape Navigator, and sophisticated Web-authoring packages whose names and features change daily. The newest iterations are always reviewed and rated in the computing periodicals.

There are many excellent HTML reference books available—cruise your local bookstore and select the one that looks the least forbidding to you, because that's the one that will be of the most use as you get started. For the motivated and stingy, there are also many HTML tutorials available on the Web, free for the downloading. (In fact, Laura has written one herself *pro bono publico*.) See Appendix B for a list of online resources, including tutorials.

There's a good deal to be said for learning enough HTML to do fast fixes to your pages. Most experienced Web authors prefer to do their own coding—inevitably the authoring programs give you something that you absolutely didn't want. It's nice to be able to go in and make your page behave.

Word-Processing Software

You can create your page, HTML codes and all, using your favorite word-processing package. But for a browser to read it, it must be saved as a text file. Most of the Windows-based word processors offer that as an option in the "save as" dialog box from the pull-down menu. (If you're still hanging on to your old WordPerfect 5.1, you can "SAVE AS DOS" with the CTRL-F5, 1, 1 sequence, but be prepared: it's a slow conversion.) You can also build files with your computer's text editor (Notepad or

Wordpad in Windows, SimpleText on the Mac), although these text editors lack many of the amenities that make word processing easier.

Internet Access

Yikes! you may wonder, *how do I get access to the Internet?* If your library already has its own Web site, it may be a simple matter of talking with your systems administrator. If your library depends on a local nonprofit (or for-profit) Internet service provider for e-mail access, that provider may offer server space as part of the service. Here in Philadelphia, we have an Internet service provider for local nonprofits called LibertyNet that provides e-mail and modest Web server space to bona fide nonprofits for an annual fee of $30, including all the communications software you need to get started. You may find a similar project in your area. Failing that, you may rent space from a commercial server.

If your organization subscribes to America Online or CompuServe, it already has server space as part of the subscription package. Both services provide online support to walk you through the process.

Access to a Scanner

Somewhere along the line, you may want to acquire a scanner and image manipulation software such as Adobe Photoshop. With scanners becoming less and less expensive, they may well enter the realm of home-office equipment in the near future.

However, you don't need to run out and buy a scanner to get started. There are other options. You might get someone on your board or one of your Friends to donate one. You may have a colleague, family member, or volunteer with access to a scanner who can provide you with the images you need for a starter site. Some reprographics houses are offering scanning services. Some photoprocessors are now offering a disk with scanned images as an add-on to traditional developing and printing. If you're willing to ask around and finagle a little, you may be able to stave off the purchase of a scanner for some time.

Simple Design Tips for Your First Set of Pages

There are as many opinions about good design on the Web as there are Web designers, and just about every Web designer will be only too happy to share his or her opinions with you. Here are the design considerations we think most useful—although we feel that content trumps all rules and so we break them when we need to.

Keep your home page simple.

Surfers want fast response time when they make the initial contact with your site, and they'll be happiest if they get a fast-loading page that lets them start their site exploration quickly. Most surfers would prefer not to have to scroll while they're looking for the right page; if you can keep your home page compact enough to fit on the old standard 640 × 480 pixel screen, so much the better. Look for tips on making a page load more quickly, and test your page on a slow modem before announcing it.

Subsidiary pages can have longer content.

If your home page links to a page or pages that also serve as "menu" pages, you'll want to keep them simple as well. When the page's primary purpose is *navigation,* try to keep it short. When its primary purpose is *to deliver content,* it can be longer. Remember, too, that surfers who visit a library site expect to find something to read there.

Have a response option on every page.

The beauty of the Web is that it encourages interaction between creator and reader. Make sure that each page contains a device that lets the reader contact you. It can be as simple as a link that provides an e-mail form, or it can be a complex and sophisticated feedback form or questionnaire.

Provide a consistent set of navigational tools.

For a small site, a simple link back to the home page will serve your navigational needs. If you are building a site with multiple sections, each page should contain a consistent set of links (graphic or textual, or both) to the major subsections.

Remember the text-only surfer.

A growing number of surfers are turning off the images when they use a modem to access the Web. When they've surfed to a page with image content they'd like to see, they load the images for that page only. Be mindful of the needs of these users and provide a text-only alternative to any critical information that you've displayed graphically.

Use the Web as your tutorial.

Another beauty of the Web is that you can steal just about everything you can see. "Stealing" is a metaphor: by saving the document to your hard drive or using your browser's "view source" feature, you can examine the HTML coding that produced it so that you can produce comparable effects. If you find icons or other artwork that appeal to you, you can save them to your hard drive by right-clicking your mouse button and, if the site owner is amenable, you can then use them in your own work. (There is usually a link to the site maintainer, so asking for permission is fairly easy; without exception, site maintainers have been happy to grant us permission to use materials.) There are also many sites offering public-domain icons, buttons, bars, and other artwork.

Cracking the Code: HTML Demystified

Most people look at a document marked up with hypertext markup language (HTML) and get a little queasy; it's full of cryptic abbreviations contained within angle brackets and it bristles with forward slashes. How will I ever remember all that, you wonder—and why should I?

We would argue that you should develop at least a minimal competence with HTML for all the same reasons that you learned long division: it's good for you and many times it's easier to go in and tweak than to mess with an HTML editor. Once you know a little HTML, though, we have no objections if you choose to use an HTML editor instead. Netscape is building an excellent suite of Web authoring tools into the "Gold" versions of its browsers (which, by the way, are still free to nonprofits), and there is an easy-to-use manual by Alan Simpson, with a CD full of useful companion software, available in most bookstores (Alan Simpson, *Official Netscape Navigator Gold 3.0 Book,* Netscape Press, 1996). Microsoft has created add-ons to convert Microsoft Word documents to HTML, as well as more sophisticated authoring tools.

You can find HTML primers online or at your local bookstore. When you've found one or two primers, these few simple concepts will help you make sense of what you read: the language is code based, the codes are contained within angle brackets, and most (but not all) of the codes come in pairs—one code to turn an action on and another—often the same code preceded by a forward slash (/)—to turn it off. This is very similar to WordPerfect in "reveal codes" mode, except that here you have to type the code yourself instead of pressing a function key.

Although the official HTML specifications group them differently, you may find HTML easier to grasp if you think of it as having three groups of codes:

- *Formatting codes* control how a document is displayed on the page and include things like boldface, italics, indentation, bulleted or numbered lists. If you wanted to put the word **library** in boldface in your HTML document, for example, you would type library.

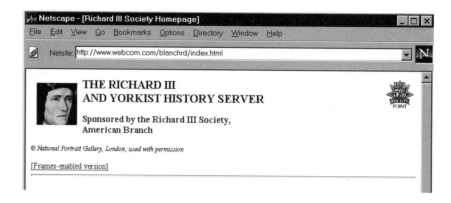

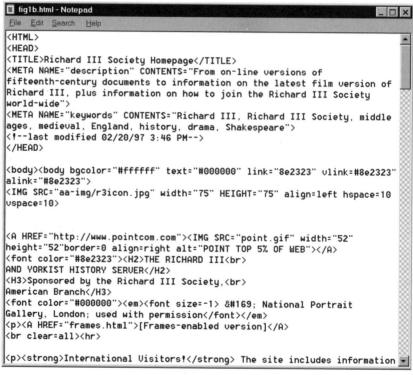

The scariest-looking bits of HTML coding are usually at the front of the document. Once you learn a "vocabulary" of about twenty codes, though, this formidable collection of angle brackets and quotation marks becomes remarkably easy to read.

- *Image codes* instruct the browser to fetch an image file and display it within your document. A single code, not a pair, is all that's required, and a bare-bones image code looks like this: <IMG SRC= "mypicture.gif">. Within the angle brackets, you can also specify image dimensions, "white space" around the image, and the position of the image on the page relative to your text. These more complicated codes may look like this: <IMG SRC="mypicture.gif" width="100" height="200" align=left hspace="10" vspace="10" ALT="mypicture">. All the numbers in quotation marks in this example refer to numbers of pixels; the rule of thumb is 72–75 pixels per inch, which is the standard screen resolution. The terms hspace and vspace refer to the number of pixels of "white space" around the image horizontally and vertically. ALT=mypicture tells the browser to display the word "mypicture" if the user has the images turned off.

- *Linking codes* instruct the browser to retrieve another file and display it in the browser window. If I wanted to link to the University of Pennsylvania Library Web site, for example, the code I would include would be <A HREF="http://www.library.upenn.edu"> University of Pennsylvania Library</A>. What does "A HREF" stand for? A genuine geek will tell you it means *argument hypertext reference,* but we find it more useful if less accurate to think of it as an abbreviation for "a link."

Remember, too, that the Web is your tutorial. You can view the HTML source code for any document by using the "view source" command located in the "view" pulldown menu.

Getting the Picture

If push comes to shove, you can put together a graphically pleasing starter site with nothing but text and some navigational icons you've downloaded from a public domain site or from a private site with the owner's permission.

But there's no question about it: your site will be much more appealing with illustrations. Photos can help you put a human face on your organization and its patrons; they bring recognition to staff, donors, and volunteers; they offer a testimonial to the vitality of your events. Photos and artists' renderings can combine to educate, inform, and persuade on behalf of your current and contemplated projects.

Ideally, you will be able to purchase a top-of-the-line flatbed color scanner and a powerful image manipulation package such as Adobe Photoshop (you'll need a powerful computer, though: at least 32 MB of memory [64 MB is better] and a fast processor). But what if the $1,500 to $2,000 for scanner, software, and upgrades isn't in the cards right now?

Fortunately, you have some options. If you're not too proud to beg, you may find someone with access to a scanner who can prepare a few images for you to get you started. We personally know of three libraries in our area that have had entire sites (including images) done for them by members of their Friends organizations. Your board, if you have one, may include a member with scanner access. (If you're really lucky, your board will include a member who will buy you a scanner!) If you have a local nonprofit Internet provider (like our LibertyNet in Philadelphia), they may be able to help you out. Some reprographics houses are starting to offer self-service scanning stations by the hour. Others will do the scanning for you, for a fee. Laura recently tested photos-on-diskette that came along with her traditional prints from her supermarket photofinisher for an extra five bucks; while she prefers her own scans, she says these aren't at all bad.

You can also manipulate images and computer graphics with a relatively inexpensive shareware program. We've downloaded PaintShop Pro and tested it on a 486 with 8 MB of RAM running Windows 3.11. We wouldn't want to have to manipulate large images with this equipment configuration, but for photos the size you'd want to put on the Web it works just fine, and it allows for a fair degree of manipulation and special effects. You can download an evaluation copy for no charge from *http:// www.jasc.com*—registration for the version we downloaded, at this writing, is a very reasonable $69.95. Many of the techniques you develop playing around with PaintShop Pro can be used if and when you move up to Adobe Photoshop.

It's important to remember that graphics files are comparatively large. A 30 KB text file will run for several pages when printed out; a 30 KB image file may fill only a few square inches. Especially on your introductory pages, you want to make sure you don't add so many images that the page takes minutes to load.

For a brief time, it was fashionable to have a home page that was one large image map, that is to say, clicking on different areas on the image would link to different pages. These home pages took excruciatingly long to load; and, to add insult to injury, the text-only surfer saw nothing but the word "IMAGEMAP" in brackets. Happily, this fashion passed quickly as its drawbacks became evident. The large clickable image can be an important tool in a library development site—especially for a virtual tour of a planned new space—but it should not be on the first, or possibly even the second, page a surfer clicks into.

There are several useful ways to work around the problem of images slowing page loading time. They include:

- Putting in the image size in pixels in the image tag. This lets the browser lay out all the textual elements around a space reserved for the image instead of waiting for the image to load before displaying text. (Some HTML editors, such as the editing feature in Netscape Navigator Gold, do this automatically.) The surfer can start reading while the images load.

- Making certain that you are saving in the fastest-loading file format for that image. Some images are saved more effectively as .gif (short for CompuServe Graphics Image Format) images, some as .jpg (short for Joint Photographic Group) images.

- Setting up your HTML file so that a low-resolution "placeholder" image loads almost immediately, followed by a slower-loading, higher-resolution version.

- Putting in a small version of the image, with a link to a larger version for those who are willing to wait for the larger image to load.

Getting It All Online

You can build your entire site right on your hard drive, but eventually you will need to put it on the World Wide Web. This can be a complicated process, but it can also be remarkably easy. Netscape Navigator 3.0 Gold has a push-button publishing function. If you have chosen an Internet provider that accepts their publishing function (and Netscape has a list of them, available in the "Creating Net Sites" section of its Web site), it's as simple as point, click, and upload. It's not much harder to upload traditionally with Windows or Mac, either: there are shareware programs (WS_FTP for Windows and Fetch for Mac) that are a real pleasure to use.

If your library has its own Web server, you'll need to consult with your systems administrator. She may want you to become minimally proficient with the UNIX operating system—for many fledgling Web authors this is pretty scary, but it actually only involves learning a handful of unintuitive commands. Or, you may be able to hand off files on a diskette and have someone else upload them.

In chapter 8, we'll look at taking your site beyond the basics.

8

Developing
Your Site

In the previous chapter we took a look at what's involved in building a basic site—hardware, software, and expertise. Very quickly, though, you'll want to move beyond these basics.

Much of the growth of your site will involve becoming more familiar with the tools just described. As you learn more about HTML itself, for example, you'll learn how to control the colors of your text and your backgrounds, to control your typeface, and to work around the limitations of HTML to create pleasing layouts. An investment of a few hours spent playing with your image-manipulation software will yield important dividends: you'll be able to blend images into collages, for example, or combine visual and textual elements in one image file that can then be mapped and used as a navigational tool. These are extensions of topics covered in the previous chapter, and ones you can explore on your own.

In this chapter, we'll concentrate on three areas. We'll look at ways to make your site more interactive and to encourage communication from your audience. We'll offer some thoughts on the added dimension that audiovisual materials can bring to your online presentation. Finally, we'll talk about how to set your site in the context of an overall site for your library, to keep it up to date, and to develop measures for assessing the success of your efforts.

Making Your Site Interactive

No matter how simple you decide to make your initial site, one absolute essential is some way in which your readers can interact with you. The irreducible minimum is the "mailto"—a hypertext link that displays a preaddressed e-mail form. We have one at the end of each page on our Penn Library Friends site. It takes advantage of one of the real beauties of the Web, the fact that responding electronically is even easier than filling out a prepaid postcard. You can make this link stand out by adding a button or other icon, like the "tell me more" buttons we've sprinkled around our site near the projects still in need of that special major donor.

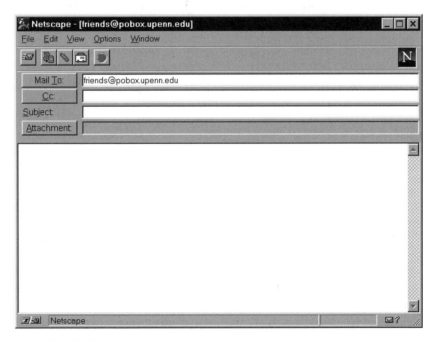

A "mailto" link

The next step up from the "mailto" link is the form. The reader clicks on a link, a form pops up, she fills out the information and sends it on its way, receiving a confirmation from the server that the message has been sent. Some uses include:

Signing Up New Friends

Fill out an online membership form, select a level of giving, push the send button and, voila! instant Friend. We start your membership immediately and bill you.

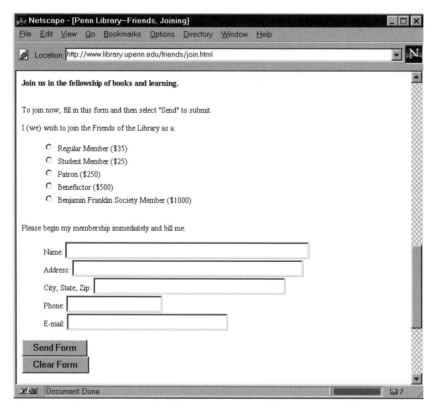

It's easy to become a Friend of the University of Pennsylvania Library.

Collecting Pledges

We want to catch those donors in the instant that their emotions are engaged, and a form such as the one shown below allows them to act on their generous impulses immediately. Eventually, we'll offer credit card or digital cash payment options—for now, we're content to bill our donors. This has not been a particularly active form for us, and to be quite honest, we didn't expect it to be in the early days when most surfers weren't making the connection between online activity and charitable gifts. What it did communicate was the fact that there was a need for contributions and an active campaign going on.

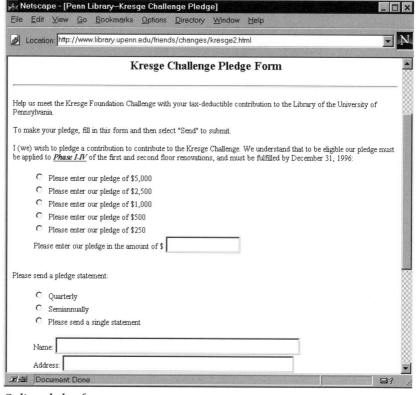

Online pledge form

RSVPing for an Event

As more and more of your stakeholders join the wired world, this becomes an easy and convenient means of accepting reservations for an event. We tested the concept at our Homecoming Showcase event in November 1996 and found that our wired Friends got a kick out of sending in their reservations electronically.

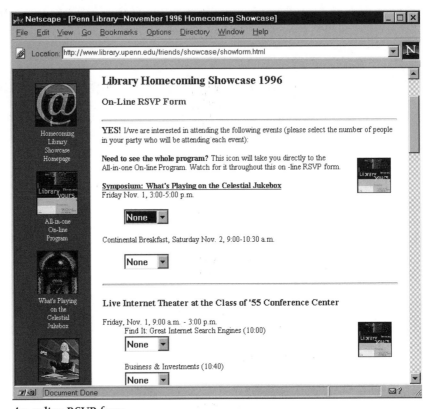

An online RSVP form

Quizzes, Surveys, Information-Gathering or Involvement Activities

Last fall we held an Internet scavenger hunt for Penn students—the prize was a Pentium computer with all the trimmings. Library Friends could join in the Web hunt fun from their own computers with an online quiz—if they got a certain number of the questions right, they received a "Great Web Hunt" pin and other small prizes.

You can use similar forms to survey your members, gather opinions on important issues, offer similar contests—or any of a dozen other ways to engage them in a dialog. As we mentioned in an earlier chapter, you can even use a form to sign up volunteers.

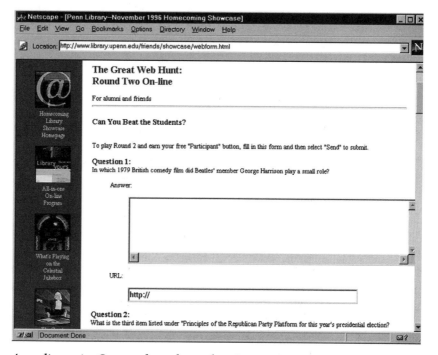

An online quiz: Can you beat the students?

Creating Your Form

There are two parts to creating a form, only one of which is under your control. The part you can control is creating the form itself: most of the HTML manuals and several online guides will show you the coding and offer you an array of tips. The second part is under the control of your site administrator. Each form is paired with a script that resides in a special directory on the server. When your reader fills out the form and pushes the "submit" button, this script is used to process the information contained in the form and pass it along to your e-mail account, to a database, or to some other information repository.

Creating those scripts is fairly technical, and making an error in a script can cause security problems on your server, so your site administrator will most likely have to create it for you. If you are renting space from a commercial or a not-for-profit Internet service provider, you will need to consult with them to find out whether they support forms and what the procedures are.

The All-Singing, All-Dancing Site

We've already argued that the "entertainment-rich" site niche should be filled by someone other than the Friends of the Library. After all, why compete with Disney and MGM?

On the other hand, you may have a topic that cries out for more of a multimedia approach. Our Marian Anderson centennial celebration is a case in point. It was also the project that moved us to acquire some multimedia equipment. Earlier we mentioned how we celebrated Marian Anderson's 100th birthday by expanding our online exhibition, "Marian Anderson: A Life in Song" (*http://www.library.upenn.edu/special/gallery/anderson/*). The audiovisual material consists of two video clips, including one of her landmark Lincoln Memorial concert; three songs, including the world premiere of her 1936 recording of Jean Sibelius's "War det on dröm"; and eight interview excerpts in which Miss Anderson discusses critical turning points in her life.

You can produce acceptable-quality Web video if your machine has a video capture card, a sound card, and some horsepower. The video capture software comes with the video capture card; once you've spent $300 or so for the two cards, all you need is a VCR and some cables. Audio capture is also reasonably inexpensive; a cassette player or CD player and some cables, plus a $50 shareware program downloaded from the Web, will get you started. If you want to go into video editing in a bigger way, you'll want to think about acquiring a more sophisticated program, such as Adobe Premier.

The two obstacles to audiovisual extravaganzas, at least at this writing, are bandwidth issues and cross-platform issues. "Radio-quality" audio, which means AM radio, eats up .5 to 1 MB per minute. Video compressed to fit even a small window is even more demanding—between 6 and 10 MB per minute. If you are renting server space by the megabyte, each video clip could conceivably add $10 or $15 to your monthly site rental. If your audience mostly lives in modem-land, you have to ask yourself how many of them are going to wait an hour for a two-minute clip to download. The other concern is finding the format that is most likely to be accessible to your audience. If your surfer doesn't have the appropriate software to view or listen to the clip, you will need to include links to a site from which the software can be downloaded.

Despite these obstacles, audiovisual components can add an exciting extra dimension to your site, if you have a constituency that is likely to be able to make use of them. If many of your stakeholders have ethernet

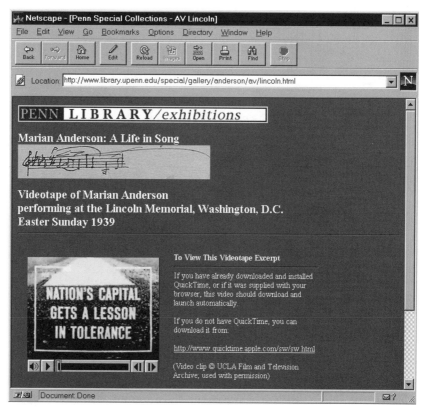

It takes Apple QuickTime Video to view this video clip, so the page includes a link to Apple's downloading site.

access, or if you plan to distribute your Web site on a Web-enabled CD, by all means consider adding sound and motion. For more on the advantages of putting your content on a CD, see chapters 10 and 11.

Publicizing Your Site Where It Counts

Publicizing your site to the wide world is fairly easy. You navigate to the home pages of the major search engines, click on the icon or text line that says "submit URL" or "submit new site," and follow the instructions.

More important to you, though, is reaching those surfers who are coming to visit your library's site, since these people are more likely to become your Friends, advocates, donors, and volunteers than the world at large. To bring this about, you want to cross-connect with the rest of your library's site at as many points as possible. Here are a few:

Your Library's Home Page

As we write, we have a link from the Penn Library's home page pointing to our site and labeled "Friends of the Library." We're in the process of updating our site and its name to reflect its broader purpose. Yes, we're about the Friends of the Library and the benefits of membership in that group. But we're also about the library's plans for the future, its staff resources, its named funds for books and other materials, its many benefactors, and—an overarching theme—its strategy for meeting the changing information needs of the university community as we approach the twenty-first century.

We're really about a lot of things that don't have all that much to do with membership in the Friends of the Library. Our new name will reflect this broader theme. As you name your own section of your organization's Web site, think about what you name it and whether those few words on your organization's home page will draw your entire audience to your pages.

Other Cross-Connections

Consider the rest of your library's site and lobby for connections wherever you see a possibility. Some of ours at Penn include:

- cross-linking a donor recognition site with the Web section for the department in which the donor's project resides;
- asking for a link from the "What's New" page for any news of events, new gifts, etc.; and

having a link from the Special Collections department to the Friends portion of your site.

If your library maintains an online calendar of library events, this would be an ideal place to cross-link your Friends events with your pages.

Keeping Your Site Fresh

There's a new term coming into vogue in the Web development world: *dead sites*. Dead sites are the ones that are launched with great enthusiasm and then not maintained. You can spot them by their large numbers of broken links, their "last updated" notations more than a year old, their calendars whose most recent entry was August 1995.

Happily, a little preventive maintenance can keep your site current—or at least not looking woefully dated. Here are some suggestions:

Remove the "Last updated" line from the bottom of your pages.

You can keep updating information behind the scenes in your HTML document with a comment that tells you (and the search engines) when the page was last modified. At our site, we're replacing those "last updated" footers with a simple line saying "this page maintained by *friends@ pobox.upenn.edu*"—and making the e-mail address a hotlink. One of the difficulties of a "last modified" date in public view is that you may update a page and forget to update that date. Your fresh page winds up looking like last week's news.

Take down your "Events" pages as soon as the events are over.

Our "Library Showcase" event was November 1–2, 1996. The pages were de-linked on November 3, although we left them on the server so that anyone following old links from another page outside our site would not encounter a "file not found" message. The pages still offer links to the rest of our site and to more current information.

Keep a list of time-sensitive pages, and put their update dates on your planning calendar.

This isn't foolproof, but it will help. Periodic checks of the pages on the list in addition to making changes as they come up on your calendar will go a long way to keeping you out of the "old news" trap.

Surf your site looking for "link rot."

This wonderfully descriptive phrase refers to those cases where another site you've linked to has moved or killed the page, leaving your surfers with an error message instead of the page they expected. This is particularly important if you're linking to someone else's time-sensitive pages. The other site maintainer may be scrupulous about removing outdated material, leaving your links hanging.

These techniques are all negative—that is to say, they're ways to keep your site from looking dated. Our last tip is far more positive:

Put your hottest news at the top of your home page.

When U.S. Chief Justice William Rehnquist declared Richard III not guilty in a mock trial at Indiana University in October 1996, that was hot news. When word reached the Richard III Society that the trial would be broadcast on C-SPAN in January 1997, that was hot news, too. Both were featured in the top news spot on the organization's home page

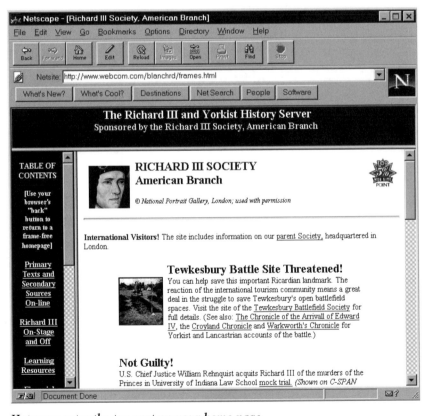

Hot news rates the top spot on your home page.

(*http://www.r3.org/*). Although it has been superseded by other news, Richard III's acquittal is still intriguing enough to merit a prominent spot in the organization's home page. Less-hot news can go on your "what's new" page.

We gave the same "top billing" to our Penn Library Showcase event on November 1–2, 1996—and made sure we took it off November 3.

If you're featuring hot news on your home page, it's especially crucial to do site maintenance to keep your home page current. Mark your calendar; set your alarm—but get the old news off the minute it gets old!

Measuring the Impact of Your Site

It would be nice if you could count up the online pledges, measure them against the cost of building and maintaining a site, and use that as the measurement of your site's impact. It probably won't be that simple, but here are some quantitative and qualitative measures you can use to evaluate the return on your investment in the Web. We'll use Laura's Richard III Society site as a whimsical example, interspersed with insights from some of the other sites she maintains.

Access Reports

Many Internet service providers make reports available to their customers. Laura gets a daily report for her Richard III Society site that tells her the total number of file requests, the total number of accessors, the number of hits per file, and the activity for each accessor (the server from which their request originated, and a list of files they requested). If challenged, she could tell you that in the month of January 1997 the site received 55,742 file requests from 4,826 individual accessors, and that the most popular pages, after the home page, were the ones on the Al Pacino documentary on Richard III.

The University of Pennsylvania Library makes a monthly summary available to its Web developers, with information for each day, weekly totals, and totals for a bewildering variety of categories and subcategories such as type of browser and whether the image display function was turned on or off. These data are very important to a Web development staff preoccupied with cross-browser compatibility.

Over at the nonprofit Internet service provider, LibertyNet, Laura gets a monthly access report for the site for the Philadelphia Area Consortium of Special Collections Libraries, showing a breakdown of the files requested and the number of unique accessors.

Whether you get a detailed report or a summary, these access reports will help you determine how effectively your site is publicized—that is to say, how many people visit any page on the site—and how engaging your site is to its visitors.

Feedback from the Site

You can collect both quantitative and qualitative data from reader response to your feedback devices—"mailto" links and forms. Laura can tell you, for example, that she receives on average three inquiries a day from the Richard III Society site. Usually two of them are from baffled high school students trying to find online references for a research paper—so she knows that the site is fulfilling its primary purpose as an educational resource for students. The remaining inquiries are usually also research questions from the general public.

Laura also receives regular reports from the membership chairman on renewals and new memberships. Members who join from the Web print out an online application form and in consequence are very easy to track—so Laura knows that two or three new members join each week as the result of the Web site. At $30 per member, this represents $300 to $400 in new revenue each month, easily five or six times what the Society spends on the site.

Back at Penn, we're just beginning to put our E-Friend button all over our site. It's too soon for us to sit back and count the E-Friends, but stay tuned.

Comments from Your Stakeholders

A good development site does more than recognize donors or garner online pledges. It validates the organization's vision and communicates it in a clear and compelling way to a variety of stakeholders, engaging the viewer and encouraging a two-way conversation between Web developer and reader. If you've done your job properly, you'll be hearing from those stakeholders—your patrons, your colleagues, your volunteers, and your donors. Be sure to save the glowing tributes you receive from delighted Friends and colleagues (and be assured, you *will* receive them). They are eloquent testimony to your site's ability to engage not only the attention but also the emotions of its visitors.

9

Players on a Web Team

We currently can envision the basic Web package for a development team as consisting of three components:

1. An identifiable Web site that contains basic information about your institution—and the ability to change and improve your site whenever you are ready;

2. Interactive capabilities lodged in your site, so that constituents and visitors can communicate with you, can do business with you, and possibly can communicate with each other;

3. Web-based publications, such as donor books, limited-run brochures, color printed project descriptions, and so on.

To get started on the Web, it is not necessary to have all the hardware, software, and staff expertise as an in-house resource. Almost everything you need to do can be "farmed out" to service providers if you want to start that way, or can be a shared resource with other units.

If you want to run your own show, then you will need to devote resources to equipment and staffing. We have covered equipment needs in chapters 7 and 8. Your biggest investment, however, will be staff time.

In fact, if present predictions hold true, our future Web browser will become the gateway for everything we do on our computers—whether we are operating "locally" (on our machine) or globally. We may not even think of such a thing as a "Web browser," but simply use our standard computer interface to take us wherever we want to go.

As Web editing and management software gets easier, and Web use becomes more widespread, all of us in development and public relations will eventually acquire authoring, design, and even administrative skills, in much the same way that many of us currently have some level of competence in word processing, database management, and spreadsheeting.

In that glorious day, perhaps not far off, we may not need any specialized staff on our payroll. But that's Tomorrow. For Today, this is what you need:

Webmaster

Someone, somewhere, has to be able to mount, maintain, fix, and upgrade the Web server software that supports your system. This is a highly technical job, requiring a variety of computer skills, including programming. At the Penn Library, our Web server is maintained by the Systems staff. Other schools and units at Penn have their Webmasters and Web managers. And there are technical people who maintain the main Web pages for the university, to which we all link.

If you intend to maintain your own Web server, then you need a Webmaster, or Web "manager." We confess to liking the first term, since it has a more medieval/science fantasy quality, and has already led to the formation of a professional association called "The Guild of Web Masters." (The term *webgoddess* is an attractive alternative for some.)

A Webmaster is someone who might *conceivably* make sense of the following passage, taken somewhat at random from an article in the August 1996 issue of *Byte* magazine:

> You value a common object-oriented language for components and glue. OOP fans have rightly pointed out that VBX and OCX components sacrifice inheritance for reuse. The same is true for their successors, ActiveX components.

Got that? No? Then it would be better not try to be your own Webmaster.

Hiring a Webmaster nowadays is a bit difficult. Everyone wants a Web site, every Web server needs a Webmaster. A classic sellers' market. We believe that most systems offices are training existing staff to manage Web sites. Talk to your systems administrator if your organization does not already have a site and see what she has in mind. If you don't have a systems office, then hire an outside vendor to mount and manage your Web page and the vendor will worry about hiring suitable *meisters*.

Site Designer

A site designer is similar to a graphic designer, and there are freelance designers who can craft your site under your direction. Just supply the text and images, and they will take it from there. (Search under "Web design services" for a list of such professionals.) Once the overall look of your pages is determined and the site created, you may be able to maintain and even extend the site with minimal assistance.

It is not essential to have a designer when you first create your site. Web pages can be created and mounted on a server with relative ease, and a basic page, with graphics, is within the ability of most people who can do word processing. A bit of training or a good manual may be helpful. Keep in mind that you can create your pages, and look at them, and edit them—all on your hard drive, and without releasing them to the world. Only when you are satisfied with your creation will you transfer the files to the Web server. (See chapters 7 and 8 for do-it-yourself tips.)

A workable strategy is to create a set of basic, plain vanilla pages, and then improve them over time. Designate someone to get additional design training, and let that person enhance your pages as part of his learning experience. Have that pioneer share ideas and tips with the rest of your staff, so that you all slowly acquire greater proficiency. If you decide on an enhancement that is beyond your staff's capacities, it is possible to hire a freelancer for specific tasks, such as creating a few forms with CGI (Common Gateway Interface) script.

Web Maintainer

Once you have your site up, you will need someone on your staff who can maintain the site. That is a simpler task than design. A maintenance person needs the skills to transfer files back and forth between his computer and the server. He needs to be able to edit Web pages, check them for quality, and send them back to the server for inclusion.

Web sites require constant maintenance. "Upcoming Events" become past events, "special offers" start looking not-so-special, "News" becomes stale, fees change, dates change, pictures can be replaced, new information can be added and updated. This kind of Web work requires a minimum of skill, and someone in your shop should be designated to play this role. An important part of the role is to undertake a routine "check" of your site to see that links work, pictures load, forms function, etc. A test cruise once a week is a good idea, or at least once a month.

Web Monitor

If your Web site has interactive aspects—forms that can be filled out and sent, "mailtos" that allow the viewer to send comments, online membership and pledge forms—then you need to designate a person or persons who will receive these messages and take action on them. On the Internet, people expect a fairly rapid response. Your monitor should be prepared to send a "we received your submission" message right away, and then to make sure that a full response is posted in short order.

Web Writer

Even though it is graphical, the Web still demands a fair amount of text. You will need writers for donor recognition pages, newsletters, guided tours, gift "opportunity" pages, announcements, and so on. Fortunately, anyone who can create a word-processed document can be a writer for your pages. Web editing software can take such documents and convert them to Web documents in a flash—in Microsoft Word it can be as easy as selecting "save as" and then selecting "html document."

But if that is too much for your writers, who may be Web-blocked, just ask them to give you the document in any standard format. And make sure they keep their text short. Long text on the Web can be a killer.

Don't be intimidated by all these tasks, however. When we first got started, Laura was the Web-everything: designer, monitor, maintainer, and writer. And she was a half-time employee. We got a pretty good site going with this investment of staff time, and so can you.

10

Beyond Bandwidth: The Web-Enabled CD

At the Penn Library we have been experimenting with the publication of our online pages on a CD-ROM disc for distribution far and wide. This is a relatively new concept which some people are referring to as a "Web-enabled CD."

The University of Pennsylvania Library Online Sampler

During Homecoming 1996 the library distributed 1,500 copies of the *Sampler* CD free to alumni and visitors. The disc contains the full text and images from four "online exhibits" that have been mounted on the Web by the Library's Special Collections Department.* *The University of Pennsylvania Library On-line Sampler,* as the experimental disc is called, has been designed so that it can be "read" using any standard Web browser, allowing home users to view large graphic files at high-bandwidth speeds.

In addition to the four online exhibits, we include a significant portion of the library's "Visions" site—in other words, our "pitch" for the library's plans and dreams. An eight-panel insert describes the offerings and gives credit to the many people who created the contents and made the disc possible. The panel also contains careful instructions for how to access the disc.

---

*The four high-graphics exhibitions are: *Household Words: Women Write from and for the Kitchen; Bibliotheca Schoenbergensis: Selected from the Collection of Lawrence J. Schoenberg; Robert Montgomery Bird: Writer and Artist;* and *John W. Mauchly and the Development of the ENIAC Computer.* These exhibitions, and several new offerings, can be viewed at *http://www.library.upenn.edu/special/events.html.*

The disc contains many "live" Internet connections which take the viewer to other library pages and other Penn pages. It contains an electronic "form" that allows the viewer to sign up as a Friend of the Library and receive the first year of membership free. The reader handily completes the form on the disc, and when he or she clicks "send," it is automatically posted as an e-mail to our office. Similarly, there are "comments" lines at the bottom of key pages. Simply click and the reader can send an e-mail question or comment to our publishing team.

Since Homecoming, we have taken the discs on the road with us when we visit alumni clubs. Invariably, every disc is taken home by interested alumni, all of whom seem to have friends or family with Internet access and a browser even if they themselves do not.

The *On-line Sampler* disc works on both the Mac and Windows platforms. The viewer navigates the disc just as he or she would any Web site. This is a simple but powerful electronic publishing concept, and surprisingly, one that is just beginning to catch on.

The first advantage of this new publishing technique is that the material is right there on the disc, ready to use. The reader does not have to search through hundreds of thousands of sites to find the exhibitions. So: you have "instant find."

The second advantage is that the pictures will load very quickly. For people who are used to accessing the Web with 14.4 or 28.8 modems, the speed of access will seem miraculous. Even for those who have high-bandwidth access, the images will load as fast or faster, since they do not have to traverse the ever-more-crowded Internet. So: you have "instant bandwidth."

The third advantage is that *all links work—even those that are "off" the disc.* This means that if the exhibition has a link to another site somewhere on the Internet, when you click on the link, you will go to that site. Hit the "back" button and you are back on the disc. So: the disc acts as a "platform," or even a "trampoline," allowing the viewer to jump back and forth from "local" reading to "networked" reading.

The fourth advantage is that *everything on the disc can be read without the host machine being connected to the Internet.* That is, you can view the material without having to have an Internet account and without having to have a modem. All you need is a CD-ROM drive and a Web browser (which we intend to provide in future CDs). Furthermore, if you do not have a CD-ROM drive, a Weblike presentation can be placed on a floppy disk (though much less space is available for the presentation). So: the disc allows for a "simulated virtual Internet experience." (If this sounds like "genuine imitation leatherette," you are guilty of having read *Mad Magazine* in a former life.)

The cost of such discs is remarkably low. If an organization already has a CD-recording machine (under $500), the cost per disc is simply the cost of the blanks: about $5. Once the prototype disc is complete and ready to publish, a "master" disc is created. If the master is used to produce 500 discs or more, the unit cost drops to less than $3, depending on how fancy the packaging is. Unit costs of under $2 are achievable in runs of over 2,000. (See the next chapter for complete details on how to "burn your own disc.")

At $3 apiece you can give the disc away. You can mail it to your Friends. You can use it as a "premium." You can set it out on a table and encourage visitors to help themselves to a copy. You can make it your holiday card. Why not? It is great publicity for the library.

Or you can sell it. A "Greatest Hits" of your library or institution ought to be worth $10, maybe more. After all, with audio CDs selling at $15, you have a bargain!

Using a Web-Enabled CD-ROM

The Library Case Statement

It appears to be a truism that every major fundraising campaign requires a case statement—and the slicker the better. We confess that we sometimes wonder if this article of faith has been secretly nurtured by the printing and design industry—much as "Grandparents Day" has been created by the greeting card industry.

Astonishingly, such printed brochures can cost as much as $10 a copy, and they are often obsolete within six months of printing. Yet no major gifts fundraiser, and no high-level volunteer, wants to be caught without a classy case statement to press into a prospect's warm hands.

At the Penn Library we asked ourselves whether we could build our case statement around the Showcase CD. After all, it already contained our "Visions" pages, and it was a "must-read" for anyone who had a CD-ROM drive. Far better than a printed piece, it demonstrated that the library is at the cutting edge of information services for the twenty-first century. And it connected viewers to the much larger—and extremely impressive—main Penn Library Web site. So we have decided to "go for it," figuring that whether it is a great success or a great flop, we will at least have made a bit of history.

As this is written, we are still revising the disc for release as part of a "package" that also contains instructions and a printed brochure. We plan to introduce video clips with welcomes from the library director and the provost or president.

We also will include our full range of gift opportunities, as well as a hyperlink that will allow the reader to review the latest list on our Web site. We will have a pledge form, and a "tell me more" form on the disc.

Knowing that the demographics of major donors indicate that the younger (and less wealthy) alumni are most likely to be "networked" and that the older (and more wealthy) alumni are likely to confuse a URL with the NFL, we will hedge our bets. The disc will be part of a boxed package that contains a modest (sixteen-page) printed case statement (cover in color, rest in black and white). In addition, we will include a letter from the director that describes the package as an experiment and solicits detailed feedback. A response form will be enclosed, with a pre-paid response envelope. The library development office 800 number will also be prominently featured.

We hope that the package will be such a novelty that it will encourage investigation and that recipients will make a special effort to get a friend or family member to show them the disc, if they don't have a computer. The disc will demonstrate to computer-literate prospects that the library is on the cutting edge of the information revolution. The description of the package as "experimental," and the invitation to write, e-mail, or call with comments will not only smooth the "what-the-hell-is-Penn-sending-me-now" response, it will *engage* the reader and encourage exploration. The printed brochure will give computerless recipients something to look at, and might even be read by those who have computers—in fact, some might even *prefer* it to the disc (imagine that!).

As with a printed case statement, we do not expect our Web-CD case statement to raise money directly. Rather, it will help to prepare the way and will help to build an interested constituency. It will also give fundraisers and fundraising volunteers something pretty snazzy to present to a warm prospect. At the very least, the hoopla surrounding the package will bring attention to the library and raise its profile as a lively, innovative institution.

More on the Concept

Instant Bandwidth

Bandwidth, bandwidth, bandwidth. It's the Web's naughty little secret. The Jane and John Q. Publics, who are supposedly dying to spend hours on the Web for fun and (other people's) profit, are in fact finding the Web-cruising experience to be a bit of a drag. The primary reason is bandwidth restrictions.

Jane and John are using telephone lines and modems to access the Web, either directly through an Internet service provider, or through a service like America Online. A fast modem connection will move 28,800 bits of information per second. That sounds pretty fast, and it *is* fast for text. Theoretically, it means that a 200-word article could be transmitted in 1/100th of a second, though actual Internet transfer rates are usually much lower.

Transferring a picture, however, is another matter. The *New York Times* ran a little test for itself when its reporter was reviewing an experimental "cable modem" system in Elmira, New York. The high-speed coaxial cable modem could transfer a 3×5-inch image of Mark Twain sitting on his porch in Elmira in less than 3/100ths of a second. A standard modem, using standard phone lines, took one and one-half minutes. (*New York Times,* 1/31/96)

And that's nothing compared to moving audio and video files. For instance, there's the new Disney site (*http://www.disney.com*), containing hundreds of cartoon clips and hundreds of song snippets. Great concept! The only problem is that with a standard modem, a thirty-second cartoon might take thirty *minutes* to download. How many times will Junior Q. Public want to fool with that kind of wait before ditching the Internet and heading back to the TV?

And that is why the Web-enabled CD is "cool." *It provides instant bandwidth.* Images load as fast or faster than they would with a T1 fiber optic line, and that ain't bad. As a result, our online exhibitions can be seen at a reasonable pace, and without having to file your nails or walk the dog between images. For that reason alone, speed-starved computer owners are likely to spend time looking at what we have placed on the disc. For now, it's a cheap way to get a glimpse of what the Web is supposedly all about.

Instant Find

But browsing is not a good way to use the Web for serious projects, whether the project be finding rare book sites or finding a rare steak in Chicago.

One way to find a site is to already have the address. If a friend has already given you the URL for Chicago Steak and Fry, then all you have to do is type in "*http://www.city-life.com/chicago/restaurants/chgo_steak/ index.html*" and you are there. Provided that you wrote *the exactly correct address string* on your napkin. Miss a letter? Tough luck. Capitalize a letter that is supposed to be in lower case? Too bad. Put in a comma instead of a period? Maybe the McDonalds next to your motel will have to do.

The Web is very unforgiving of error, which is ironic since the Web itself is full of errors. Addresses must be exact. There is (as of yet) no human or automated service that relays back to you "sorry, term not found, did you mean 'chgo_steak'?"

Another way to find something is to use a Web "search engine." These searching services maintain huge databases that index Web pages in a variety of ways, including searches of every word on every page. (For a sampler of search engines, check out *http://www.search.com*. Be prepared for some advertising, which is what theoretically pays for these sites.)

Two years into the Web explosion, the lead article for the May 1996 issue of *Internet World* was called "Find It!" The cover art cleverly shows a large haystack and a computer screen displaying a small needle.

And what a haystack! The article notes that one Web search service, Digital Equipment Corporation's Alta Vista (*http://altavista.digital.com*), keeps up a database of over twenty-one million pages containing more than eight billion words. The astounding aspect of Alta Vista is that if the viewer types in a search string like "rare books," in a handful of seconds the engine will return every instance of a page that contains those two words, and every instance will be "clickable," so that the searcher can jump to each site. The *overwhelming* aspect of Alta Vista is that it will return every instance, leaving you with over 3,000 sites to check. A smaller haystack to be sure, but still a haystack.

All of these methods can be time-consuming and all too often end in frustration. When the *Wall Street Journal* asked a reporter to look at how the public was actually experiencing the Web, she wrote "While its promoters paint the Web as an Information Infobahn, angry Web users complain it seems more like the Santa Monica freeway at rush hour. It's often gridlock slow, and one of the few easy things to do on it is to get lost." (*Wall Street Journal,* 1/25/96)

From the site owner's point of view, getting found can be just as frustrating. If you want to sell flowers online, well, get in line: there are thousands of online florists, all of which promise to make the experience easy and quick. In the Yellow Pages you could name your shop AAA Florist and get an alphabetical jump on the crowd. Or you could take out a display advertisement. On the Net, commercial sites are finding that they have to resort to similar tricks, and as such devices proliferate, the Net begins to look like a highway plastered with billboards.

Creating your own CD can provide a solution to these "finding" problems, particularly for a major site like the Penn Library. The idea first began to germinate when we did a tour of Penn alumni clubs in Florida. As we showed off various library and Net sites, we were surprised to see that members of the audience were furiously writing down the addresses and asking us to pause so that they could capture the exact strings. Why not give them a floppy disk with all of the connections from our talk, we asked ourselves? They could put the disk in their machine and click on anything of interest. Then the light bulb went on. We could give them more than a hotlist; we could put a good chunk of the library right on the disk!

Do such disks become outdated? Sure. But you can always put a link to an update site, or simply reissue the disk every few months—you might even build a list of avid subscribers.

A CD also allows a bit of gentle or not-so-gentle guidance of the viewer. With a CD we can put the Development pages right up front. We can build links from other points on the disc. We can run a contest from within the Development pages, or bury something that would be of interest to particular constituents—like pictures of class reunions.

It has been said that the Web is a "pull" phenomenon—that is, that your site must attract viewers by its value. An electronic brochure adds a considerable amount of "push" to your Web strategy.

Easier Navigation

A Web browser, such as Netscape Navigator or Internet Explorer, is a graphical user interface—that is, it is a piece of software that displays pictures and allows you to use a mouse or other pointing device to navigate or "browse." In a very real way, a Web browser is only a further extension of what the Macintosh brought to the world of computing. Point, click, select; go forward, go back, go up, go down, go to selection "a," go to selection "b," and so on.

Users who are familiar with either the Mac or Windows interface will generally find a Web browser easy to use. And once they have become comfortable with a Web browser, they will find anything presented in this format easy to use.

Writing in the May 14, 1996, issue of *PC Magazine,* computer consultant Jim Seymour shares his surprise that one corporate client after another was asking him to design a Web interface for accessing in-house applications. These "Web apps" included an online order entry system, an inventory-checking system, and an expense account system—all parts of the companies' Intranet. He explains the reasoning:

> While computer enthusiasts . . . tolerate and often look forward to learning a new program, most office workers shudder at the very idea; they much prefer that any new tools added to their machines use what appears to be an old, familiar interface.

The advantage of CD-ROM publishing in the HTML format is that the Web browser has become a *universal client.* Or, if you prefer, a universal viewer, or universal reader.

Keep in mind also that once you have gone to the trouble of creating a Web site or Web pages, it is no big deal to drop these pages onto a disc. Two attractive "birds" from one HTML authoring session. Not bad.

Other Uses of This Concept

By now we hope it has become obvious that there are many interesting uses of the Web-enabled publishing concept. We have already suggested that a CD publication can be used to promote Web-based library services, to "show off" online exhibitions, and to present your case statement. Here are some other ideas:

- A library could put the entire text of one or more manuscripts on a disc. A good example might be the nineteenth-century diaries of Susan Sherman and Margaret T. Spaulding, both currently available online (*http://www.library.upenn.edu/etext/diaries*). Or Duke University's Papyrus Archive (*http://scriptorium.lib.duke.edu/#exhibits*), which contains images of 1,373 papyri from ancient Egypt. These discs could make available valuable resources for scholars to use at their workstations.

- This same sort of scholarly disc could also be distributed by the library for networked use by other libraries. The contents of the disc could be uploaded to a server, thus allowing for creation of a campus "mirror" site that would run faster on the campus Intranet. Or the disc could be used in a network disc-farm scheme for CD stations. We can imagine libraries establishing "swap" arrangements for such publications, or even selling them to each other.

- The readings for a course could be assembled on a CD. This might include images of manuscripts, works of art, comments by the professor, links to other sites of interest, and even copyrighted material (with permission or under "fair use" provisions). Such discs would be particularly useful for students who do not have direct access to a high-speed campus network—including "Virtual University" students who may be thousands of miles away.

- Web-enabled discs could be produced as companions to print publications—as we have done with this book. That way the reader can use the disc to navigate to interesting sites. Such discs could also contain extensive additional material, including full-color images that would be too expensive to reproduce in a print publication.

- Web-enabled discs could be produced *instead* of books and journals.

- Recruitment CDs could be created, just as college recruitment videos are prepared today. Such discs could contain the best of the campus Web, with pictures galore. And they could contain links to other "hot" campus sites. A prospective student could fill out an application form right on the disc and rush it off to Siwash U. by clicking "send."

- Athletics departments could produce a yearly CD for distribution or sale to diehard boosters. The disc would contain the complete schedules for all games, all sports. It could contain profiles of star athletes and golden moments from the past. The disc could also include a ticket-ordering electronic form so that viewers could purchase seats online. (See Penn's ambitious Athletics Web site as an example of a cutting-edge Web site: *http://www.upenn.edu/athletics/.*)

- Any substantial nonprofit organization could create a CD that starts with whatever has been placed on the Web and builds from there. Amnesty International, with its extensive online country-by-country human rights reports, would be a prime candidate for issuing a quarterly disc to its most active members (*http://www.amnesty.org*).

A Final Word

We trust that the discussion in this chapter has been stimulating! At present, we would strongly suggest that anyone considering publication of a CD or floppy disk start with a very basic text-and-graphics approach. Don't use the just-released version of Netscape or Internet Explorer as your standard, but go back one or two releases. The idea is to create a product that any Net cruiser can access, even Jane Q. Public, Class of '39.

If it has occurred to you that Web browsers are on their way toward becoming universal multimedia access tools, then you get a gold star. One day, in the not too distant future, we will all be publishing Web-enabled multimedia CDs, or perhaps we should say, DVDs. But for the present, stay away from cutting-edge applications and other "bells and whistles." How many calls do you want to receive from frustrated constituents, asking "How do I 'configure a viewer'?" and "What's a 'General Protection Fault'?"

In the following chapter, we will provide advice on how to cut your own CD. Just think, your first "album"!

Creating a Web-Enabled CD-ROM

You've created a fabulous site, showcasing your institution's programs and resources, celebrating donors, communicating the organization's mission. Now you want to share this site with an audience that may not have the patience to wait for it all on a 28.8 KB modem connection. What to do?

One remarkably easy way out of this dilemma is to deliver the Web on a CD. Your audience can use their own Web browsers, drawing from their CD-ROM drives instead of the Internet. It's quicker, cheaper, and easier than you probably imagine, and it's enough of a novelty to deliver a wallop on impact.

At the University of Pennsylvania Library, we used this technique in the fall of 1996 to create a sampler of four online exhibitions, together with some information on our new business library and some links to our "live" library Web site. We'd never done it before, but we managed it and lived to tell about it. You can do it too. (Trust me, says Laura: I'm somebody's grandmother. Would I lie to you?)

How We Did It

First, we "whacked" our site.

We used a program called WebWhacker, from the ForeFront Group, to capture and rename HTML files and images. WebWhacker did two very important things for us:

- It automated the page collection process, by collecting the text files and their associated image files—and renaming files where necessary—so that we did not have to concern ourselves with replicating an existing directory structure or tedious editing of filenames.

- It gave us pages that would work if the user had a "live" connection to the Internet.

We found WebWhacker very easy to use—we launched our browser in one window and WebWhacker in another, overlapping, window. To select a file for whacking, we called it up in the Netscape window, switched over to WebWhacker, and clicked on the spiderweb icon; back at Netscape, we chose the next file, and so it went. WebWhacker has other features that let you automate the selection of groups of files, but we prefer to cherry-pick. Not only is file selection easy, but it's enormously empowering (actually, a real kick!) to select files and then click on an icon of a machete and have WebWhacker do all the drudge work for us. You can download your own evaluation copy of WebWhacker from the ForeFront Group at *http://www.ffg.com/download.all.html.*

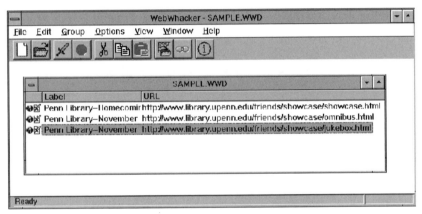

Add a page to the group by calling it up in your browser, switching to the WebWhacker screen, and clicking the Web-and-folder icon. After you've selected the pages you want to capture, click on the machete. The program captures each page and its associated image files in one directory, relinking all files and converting links to uncaptured files to full URLs.

Next, we created some new navigational pages.

In the case of our library showcase disc, we put each of our online exhibitions in its own directory within a "gallery" subdirectory and created additional subdirectories for our material about the library. We arranged our directory structure in such a way that when you chose "open file" from the pull-down menu in the Web browser there was only one file to choose—everything else was tucked away in directories or folders. Lest the user miss the point, we named that one file "welcome.htm." This file linked to a secondary "home page" for the gallery and to other introductory material. With these custom-created pages as well as the "whacked" exhibitions, we were careful to adhere to the 8.3 naming convention so that the disc would work across platforms.

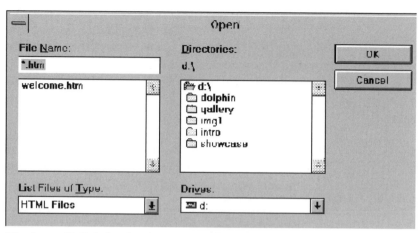

The "open file" dialog box in Netscape for Windows 3.1

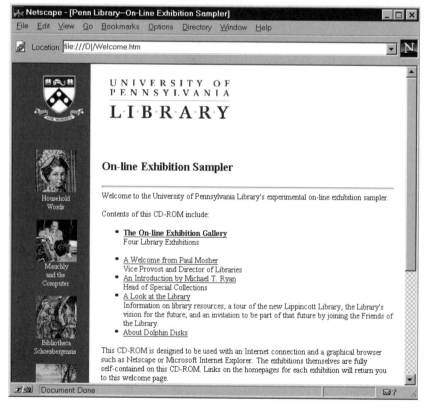

Our CD Home Page: The online exhibitions are stored in the "gallery" directory (see figure above).

Then we checked our links.

One of the perils of living with a constant ethernet hookup is that it's easy to overlook a missed page—the computer happily goes out over the Internet and retrieves it. (Remember, WebWhacker converts filenames of unwhacked pages or images to full URLs.) So we pulled the plug on our Internet connection to check our links and make sure we'd captured every page and every image we'd expected to. Invariably we would find we missed a couple, so we'd go back to WebWhacker and add them. WebWhacker automatically wove them into the materials we'd already captured.

We wanted our users to be aware that some links were to the Internet, rather than to the CD, so we dropped a little globe icon next to the "live" links. Once we had our local files linked, we plugged back in and checked the "live" links, too.

Then we transferred our files to a computer hooked up to a CD writer.

This was not a lot of fun and we would have been much happier if we hadn't had to do this, but we didn't have a CD writer of our own yet, so we had to. First, we uploaded all our files to a Web server, using FTP. This was tedious. When we were finished, we did our best to make sure they'd all made it up to the server by running through the site. Once we were reasonably sure we'd managed it, we went to another location, where a Mac was hooked to a CD writer, and downloaded all the files. This was also tedious and because we're not especially familiar with the Mac it was fraught with adventures we'd never anticipated—like the FTP program insisting that all our image files were really text files, until we rummaged in the defaults and reset some preferences. It helped that the manager of the computer lab in which we were conducting this exercise worked very closely with us and did all the major troubleshooting.

Then we checked our links again.

We found a few files that didn't make it, or that for one reason or another weren't being read properly. So we transferred those files, and checked our links again.

Then we burned the CD.

We grandmotherly types (says Laura) are easily impressed by technology, and it's pretty amazing that an appliance somewhat smaller than a waffle iron can turn out these sophisticated data storage devices. But it does. This one used a software program felicitously named "Toast." By choosing the format called ISO-9660, we created a disc that can be read almost universally—we have found one strain of aging Macintosh computers that can't read it, but it has otherwise performed well on Mac, Windows 3.1, Windows 95 and Windows NT.

Depending on what collection of equipment you are using, this part of the process will vary. But it involves running a program to "defragment" your hard drive before you start this process (something that takes about fifteen minutes), and then going through a series of steps that consumes about half an hour for the first iteration. Our 20 MB experimental CD was burned in about ten minutes—ten minutes in which a laser was making incredibly minute patterns on the disc and in which it is critical that the equipment not be jostled. We created about a half dozen of our "alpha" version for testing and evaluation. (Since burning our first CD, we've acquired our own CD writer and are happy to report that software advances have made burning an ISO-9660 CD about as hard as saving to a floppy.)

Then we checked our links, our spelling, our grammar, our syntax, and our concepts. Repeatedly.

We passed out about a half dozen of the "alpha version" to various testers, made revisions and reburned a beta, a final version, and a final-final after we found four additional small errors. Because most of the content of our CD was by now stored on the same computer as the CD writer, we transferred only the files that had been changed, speeding the process somewhat, and for the last iteration we made the changes directly on the hard drive. After each burn, though, our team of testers went through each page checking links and looking for unspotted errors. We tried to have our disc tested by folks with varying degrees of computer savvy, on different platforms (Windows 3.1, Windows 95, and Macintosh) and using various browsers (Netscape, Mosaic, Microsoft Internet Explorer, AOL). Even so, we later found that our "universal" CD did not perform well with a small number of equipment/browser combinations.

Then we sent our CD to the replicator.

Once we were satisfied that our disc was as perfect as we could make it, we sent it to a technical services firm called a "replicator." We chose a full-service house that handled CD duplication, printing for the insert booklet, assembly of our final product (jewel case, CD, insert, shrinkwrap), and that also is serving as an order fulfillment house, with a toll-free number and credit-card ordering.

The Details: What, How Much, How Long?

Here is your checklist of what you will need in order to create a CD comparable to the library's online exhibition sampler:

- ☐ Computer with fast processor
- ☐ Scanner or other means of acquiring scanned images
- ☐ Word-processing program or HTML editor
- ☐ WebWhacker or comparable software
- ☐ Internet browser (e.g., Netscape Navigator, Microsoft Internet Explorer)
- ☐ Image manipulation software (Adobe Photoshop, PaintShop Pro)
- ☐ CD writer and appropriate software
- ☐ A means to transfer large quantities of data if CD writer is not connected to the computer on which the disc contents have been created (e.g., server space and FTP software; Zip, SyQuest, or Jaz drive)

The content for our disc was created using a Dell Dimension XPS P133c computer (16 MB of memory and a 1.6 GB hard drive) with ethernet hookup and access to a Web server; a Hewlett Packard ScanJet3C color scanner, and Adobe Photoshop 3.0; no special software for HTML markup; and WebWhacker software from the ForeFront Group. With modest upgrades, this computer is now able to support a CD writer and associated software. The entire equipment configuration can be purchased for less than $8,000. (Because we did not have a CD writer or a data storage device such as a Zip drive at the time we did our first CD, we relied on server space and FTP software for data transfer. This technique greatly multiplies the potential for error and is to be avoided if at all possible.)

Replicators charge a mastering fee of $500–$2,000 depending on the quantity of CDs you order, and waive the mastering fee for the larger quantities. The cost per disc for replication, including the disc, ranges between $.60 and $.85, depending on quantity. The jewel case adds another $.30–$.35 per disc; other packaging options may raise or lower the unit cost. One of our most expensive components was the ancillary printing—four-color, eight-panel front jewel-case insert, four-color back insert, four-color silk screen on the disc itself.

Not including the time invested in creating the online exhibitions themselves, or the time of our volunteer beta testers, we estimate that the project consumed one FTE month for Laura Blanchard (Web work, interface with suppliers and printers, project management, including uncounted hours spent mastering a new skill); and about eight working days for Adam Corson-Finnerty (high concept and signing off).

The replicators can finish their part of the assignment—pressing, printing, and packaging—in two to three weeks. Based on our experience, we would suggest that you allow at least one full week between "drafts" of your CD for approvals, revisions, and reburns. Allow additional time if the drafts must be approved by someone who can't look at the disc immediately. Our production schedule is shown here as a guideline.

**University of Pennsylvania Library
On-line Exhibition Sampler CD-ROM**

PRODUCTION SCHEDULE

Insert copy to designer	Tuesday, September 10
Insert design/deadline for minor copy revisions	Friday, September 13
Proofs on inserts	Tuesday, September 17
Sign-off on CD content	Thursday, September 19
Final sign-off on printed material for negatives and match prints	Friday, September 20
Create Alpha version of disc	Monday, September 23
Create Beta version of disc	Thursday, September 26
Negatives to printer	Monday, September 30
Corrections to Beta version	Wednesday, October 2
CD Master final approval	Monday, October 7
CD Master to replicator	Wednesday, October 9
Delivery	Friday, October 25
DROP DEAD DATE	THURSDAY, OCTOBER 31

(Event Date: November 1)

Note   The individuals involved in sign-off on materials in this project were highly committed to the tight deadlines shown here. This schedule does not reflect the additional "draft version" of the CD produced and tested in one marathon session October 8. The replicator could have worked on tighter turnarounds; however, we would have incurred a rush charge.

Epilogue
The Wired Development Initiative

At Penn's Office of Library Development, most of our fundraising and communication activity is conducted in the "traditional" way: brochures, newsletters, annual appeal mailings, phone calls, personal visits, written pledge reminders, wall plaques, and bookplates. Were we to adopt an Internet-only pattern of communication, we would lose touch with the vast majority of our older constituents. This is a transitional time, and old methods must coexist with the new. However, the new methods are so revolutionary that they are transforming all forms of communication, and are leading to a new, "wired" mind-set.

As the Internet works its magic in the home, the school, and the workplace, more and more people will use it as a basic tool—like the telephone. They will use the Internet to communicate with friends, check on cultural events, play games, find sports scores, plan trips, order products, acquire information, manage their bank accounts—*and make charitable donations.*

There is a place in this matrix for your institution. The challenge is to find out where that is, and to "take your place" in a way that serves your constituency and supports your future.

We believe that libraries and other nonprofit organizations should move toward a "wired" or "Web-centric" communications model. What we mean by this term is quite simple: *Always start your communications with the Web in mind.*

Are you planning a new brochure? First, try out your written "pitch" and your design ideas on the Web. If you like what you have created, then move toward production of the printed piece. While you are waiting for the designers and the printer, your promotional piece will already be available on the Web. Perhaps you can alert your E-Friends that the brochure is there, and invite them to have a look. Perhaps you can link it to your main site, and create an electronic response form, even collect credit card gifts online. If you need a printed piece right away, you can print one or more copies of the Web-based brochure in color. If you need multiple pieces, make color photocopies of the printed Web brochure.

Often, the creation of a printed brochure is the *end* of the creative process. With a Web brochure, you may only be at the *beginning* of the creative process. For example, your brochure can be linked to additional Web material that takes the reader further into your site, or into the project that is being promoted. Thus a piece on your renovation plans can easily lead to Web pages on how the new spaces will be used, on who will use them, on what collections will be housed, what classes will be taught, and so on.

Similarly, the Web can be the beginning of planning a special event. The first notice of the event can go online, as can a registration form. Pictures, drawings, and text can be added daily. New aspects of the event can be added, and considerable background material can be linked. After the event, a photo album can be created online, and printed versions can be circulated to your guests. If something of substance happened, such as a major address, then that can be put online in text, audio, or video. In addition to promotion and education the additional value of such a lively site is that it can serve as a rallying point for volunteers and staff. Want to know what's going on? Check the event site. Want to start getting the word out early? A page can be created as soon as you have conceived of the event—and even before the event is fully planned.

A wired development office, therefore, is not an office that uses the Web exclusively to communicate with its constituency. Rather, it is an office that uses the Web to plan, organize, design, and advance an entire communications strategy. It is an office that thinks of every scrap as a potential building block, whether that scrap is a picture, a well-turned sentence, a floor plan, a drawing, a music segment, a taped interview, or a video clip. It is an office that is aware of the multipoint and multi-dimensional qualities of Web-based communications and that achieves a new synergy between print and electronic media.

The wired development office exists in cyberspace, a new dimension in which the barriers of time and distance have been largely removed, and new forms of affinity and community are possible. Increasingly, staff of the wired development office will feel comfortable soliciting, acknowledging, and stewarding electronic gifts.

We development and public relations professionals are in the midst of a process of transformation. As this transformation occurs, nonprofit institutions will find that their entire model for communication will be dramatically redrawn. The Web will change from being an interesting addition to our communications mix to being *at the very center* of our mix. The Web-centric Office. Or the Wired Office. Or simply the Modern Office.

Appendix A
Fundraiser's Choice: Cool Sites

These are some sites that we like, and which our readers will find useful and inspiring.

Note that sites do change, and some links will therefore be "dead ends"; This is unavoidable. Visit our online "Cool Sites" page at *http://www.fund-online.com/cool/* for new and updated sites.

Overall Excellence

The American Red Cross   *http://www.redcross.org*

Hey, we're not kidding. This is a knock-your-socks-off super site! Visit at length, and learn.

Official 1998 Olympic Web Site   *http://www.nagano.olympic.org*

The Olympic Movement—Home Page   *http://www.olympic.org/*

The 1996 Olympics Web site was the best we have ever seen. These two new Olympic sites are the successors of a cooperative arrangement with IBM. This just goes to show what a major sponsor and a few million dollars can do.

Creative Design

The computer museum network   *http://www.tcm.org*

The Nature Conservancy   *http://www.tnc.org/*

LibertyNet: Linking People and Information in the Philadelphia Region   *http://www.libertynet.org*

Information-Rich

Amnesty International   *http://www.amnesty.org/*

American Cancer Society   *http://www.cancer.org*

American Heart Association   *http://www.americanheart.org*

American Lung Association   *http://www.lungusa.org*

Richard III Society Home Page   *http://www.r3/org/*

Labyrinth WWW Home Page
http://www.georgetown.edu/labyrinth/labyrinth-home.html

Pledge Sites

Become a Friend of KUSM   *http://visions.montana.edu/visions/ViewersLikeYou*

Welcome to WHYY!   *http://www.whyy.org*

ReliefNet   *http://www.reliefnet.org/*

Strong Membership Emphasis

The Metropolitan Museum   *http://www.metmuseum.org*

Penn Library Friends   *http://www.library.upenn.edu/friends*

Credit Card Gifts

The Nature Conservancy   *https://www.newmedium.com/tnc/html*
    or start at the home page: *http://www.tnc.org*

American Red Cross   *http://www.redcross.org/donate/debit1.html*

Digital Cash Gifts

Working Assets   *http://www.wald.com/*

The Cyber Fridge   *http://penny.rwc.cybercash.com/kidpics*

Capital Campaign Promotion

Illinois Capital Campaign
    http://www.uif.uiuc.edu/public/Campaign/camp_toc.html

Alumni Sites

Georgia Tech Alumni Association   *http://www.gatech.edu/alumni/alumni.html*

Pitt Alumni Association Home Page
http://info.pitt.edu/~alumni/alumni/relations/alumni.html

The Association of Yale Alumni   *http://www.yale.edu/aya/*

Clever Gimmicks

The Canadian Museum of Civilization
http://www.cmcc.muse.digital.ca/cmc/cmceng/welcmeng.html

ReliefRock Home Page   *http://www.reliefnet.org/reliefrock/rock.html*

The Computer Museum Network   *http://www.tcm.org*

Donor Recognition

Marjorie I. Mitchell Multimedia Center   *http://www.library.nwu.edu/media*

The Nature Conservancy   *http://www.tnc.org/*

> Note the front page link to the Heinz Foundation.

Piers Anthony and Carol Jacob at USF-Tampa
http://www.lib.usf.edu/development/piers.html

Penn Library Benefactors   *http:www.library.upenn.edu/friends/donor.html*

Corporate Recognition

Libertynet
http://www.libertynet.org

Online Store and Sales

The Metropolitan Museum   *http://www.metmuseum.org/*

ACT UP/New York   *http://www.actupny.org/merchandise/merchandise.html*

PBS Online   *http://www.pbs.org/*

Consortial Fundraising/Public Relations

ReliefNet Home Page   *http://www.reliefnet.org/*

Philadelphia Area Consortium of Special Collections Libraries
http://www.libertynet.org/~pacscl

National Coalition for the Homeless   *http://nch.ari.net/*

Nonprofit Group Information

Meta-Index for Nonprofit Organizations
http://www.philanthropy-journal.org/plhome/plmeta.htm

> A truly monster-sized list of nonprofit organizations, and a list of lists.

Philanthropy Journal Online   *http://www.philanthropy-journal.org/*

Hunger Web   *http://www.hunger.brown.edu/hungerweb/*

Giant List of University Alumni and Development Offices
   http://weber.u.washington.edu/~dev/others.html

Nonprofit Website Directory   *http://www.contact.org/sample/dir.htm*

Action Without Borders   *http://www.idealist.org/*

Introduction to the Internet for Fundraisers
   http://www.fund-online.com/classes/internet/index.html

Impact Nonprofit Sites   *http://webcom.com/~iol/30best*

Charity Review Organizations

National Charities Information Bureau   *http://www.give.org/*

CharitiesUSA   *http://www.charitiesusa.com/*

Appendix B
The Web Developer's
Bootstrapping Toolkit

If your motivation is high and your budget is low, this collection of on-line resources will get you started in HTML authoring, Web design, and graphics for little or no expense.

HTML Authoring

A Beginner's Guide to HTML
http://www.ncsa.uiuc.edu/General/Internet/WWW/HTMLPrimer.html

A complete online primer from the University of Illinois Supercomputing Center.

A Beginner's Guide to URLs
http://www.ncsa.uiuc.edu/demoweb/url-primer.html

How to decode and link with the Uniform Resource Locators that make the Web work. Also from the University of Illinois.

Introduction to HTML and URLs
http://www.utoronto.ca/webdocs/HTMLdocs/NewHTML/intro.html
By Ian Graham, at the University of Toronto. If you like his site, buy his book.

HTML 4.0 specifications
http://www.w3.org/pub/WWW/TR/REC-html40/

This is the standard under which the World Wide Web is operating as of December 1997.

The Webmonkey
http://www.webmonkey.com/webmonkey/teachingtool/index.html

One of the finest, funniest online HTML tutorials. Includes a frames-based "monkey-see, monkey-do" feature that lets you put what you've just read into action immediately.

Softquad Home Page
http://www.sq.com/

We don't use HTML editors, but we hear this (HoTMetaL) is a good one.

Special characters in HTML
http://www.uni-passau.de/~ramsch/iso8859-1.html

> From Martin Ramsch, a listing of the character codes you need to make foreign language characters and other special symbols appear on your Web page.

Web Design and General Development Resources

Netscape's "Creating Web Sites" Section
http://home.netscape.com/assist/net_sites/index.html

> Take some time and cruise the fabulous resources Netscape has put together for Web developers. As we go to press, there's an excellent "page starter site" section here with links to many useful resources.

Microsoft's authoring/editing resources
http://www.microsoft.com/workshop/author/layout

> Additional useful authoring, design, graphics tips. Some very good material here.

Yahoo!
http://www.yahoo.com/

> Select the "computers" section from the main menu, then cruise around. You'll find online clip-art libraries, tutorials, software, a cornucopia of resources.

Web Developer Online
http://www.webdeveloper.com/

> From Mecklermedia, publisher of many Internet-related periodicals. Many fascinating links in their "resources" section.

Web Wonk
http://www.dsiegel.com/tips/index.html

> From Dave Siegal, the author of *Killer Web Sites,* some provocative and in-your-face commentary on Web design.

Designing Web Graphics
http://www.lynda.com/dwg/bookmks.htm

> Lynda Weinman has written a book and created a set of online resources.

Graphics: A Starter Kit

The Pixel Foundry
http://the-tech.mit.edu/KPT/KPT.html

> From those cutting-edge folks at MIT, lots of links to useful resources for graphics on the Web.

Online Adobe Photoshop Tutorial
http://www.duke.edu/~ac10/photoshop/index.html

> One of the best we've seen.

Paint Shop Pro
http://www.jasc.com/

> From JASC, Inc., the inexpensive shareware program that lets you draw, paint, and edit scanned images.

The World of Color

I Am Curious Yellow
http://www.upenn.edu/computing/group/dmp/technical/colors/curious.html

> Color on the Web is complicated and nothing is going to make it really easy, although some of the tools gathered here may help. This site from the University of Pennsylvania's new Media Department presents color in all of its bewildering complexity.

Non-Dithering Colors
http://www.lynda.com/hexh.html

> A swatch chart, also from Lynda Weinman. These 256 colors may not look exactly alike from monitor to monitor, but at least they'll look like colors instead of patterns.

The BEACHRat
http://www.eprise.com/hex/rgb.cfm

> If you've chosen an RGB color in Adobe Photoshop and want to convert it to the code that browsers use, BEACHRat will do it for you, automagically. Useful and wildly funny.

File Transfer

Fetch
http://www.dartmouth.edu/pages/softdev/fetch.html

> Just about the standard for Macs, developed at Dartmouth.

WS_FTP
http://www.ipswitch.com/Products/WS_FTP/index.html

> Just about the standard for Windows. So clever you can use it as a file manager, and it has a link to Notepad so you can edit and transfer files from the same window.

Miscellaneous

QuickTime
http://www.apple.com/quicktime/

> Where to download the popular video viewing software.

WebWhacker
http://www.ffg.com/

> Click that machete icon and start downloading chunks of the Web to your hard drive. From the ForeFront Group.

Online Supplement to this Resources List
http://www.fund-online.com/

> Adam and Laura keep surfing and finding new resources—they also surf and check for link rot on the resources they've listed here. Laura parked her online HTML tutorial on this site, too. Check out their latest!

Index

Adam Corson-Finnerty is Director of Development and External Affairs for the University of Pennsylvania Library. Prior to that, he served as Development Director with the Historical Society of Pennsylvania, an independent research library. Adam is one of the founders of the Academic Library Advancement and Development Network (ALADN) and speaks regularly on high-tech fundraising.

Laura Blanchard is electronic publishing specialist for the Department of Development and External Affairs at the University of Pennsylvania Library, a position she has held since early 1995, and is also the Executive Director of the Philadelphia Area Consortium of Special Collections Libraries. She comes to the field of fundraising for libraries after an early career in advertising and publishing.